The Struggle for a Decent Politics

THE STRUGGLE FOR A DECENT POLITICS

ON "LIBERAL" AS AN ADJECTIVE

MICHAEL WALZER

Yale

UNIVERSITY PRESS

New Haven and London

Published with assistance from the foundation established in memory of
James Wesley Cooper of the Class of 1865, Yale College.

Yale University Press books may be purchased in quantity for educational,
business, or promotional use. For information, please e-mail
sales.press@yale.edu (U.S. office) or sales@yaleup.co.uk (U.K. office).

The first epigraph is republished with permission of Princeton University
Press from *Sounds, Feelings, Thoughts: Seventy Poems by Wisława Szymborska—
Bilingual Edition,* translated and introduced by Magnus J. Krynski and
Robert A. Maguire, copyright 1981; permission conveyed through Copyright
Clearance Center, Inc.

The second epigraph is from "I feel good in my trousers," from *Great
Tranquility* by Yehuda Amichai. Copyright © 1982 by Yehuda Amichai.
Used by permission of HarperCollins Publishers. Reprinted by permission
from Hana Amichai.

Set in Adobe Garamond type type by IDS Infotech Ltd.
Printed in the United States of America.

Library of Congress Control Number: 2022937036
ISBN 978-0-300-26723-5 (hardcover : alk. paper)

A catalogue record for this book is available from the British Library.

This paper meets the requirements of ANSI/NISO Z39.48–1992
(Permanence of Paper).

10 9 8 7 6 5 4 3 2 1

For JBW, with whom I have been sheltering in place(s) for more than sixty years

So he wants happiness,
so he wants truth,
so he wants eternity,
just where does he get off!

—Wisława Szymborska

Even though I know I'll die
And even though I know the Messiah won't come,
I feel good.

—Yehuda Amichai

Contents

Preface and Acknowledgments

I wrote this book during the pandemic months, sheltering in place at home in Princeton, locked out of my Institute for Advanced Study office, without access to most of my books and papers. A lonely time: I worked without help from my friends—except for my closest friend, to whom this book is dedicated, and a few others with whom I managed to keep in touch. It isn't an academic book; I've given up on footnotes, and my bibliography includes only the books with which I was sheltering. It isn't a work of political theory, although I will be glad if theorists find it interesting. There is nothing systematic here. What I have written is an argument about politics—about the best kind of politics. It's not quite a program, more like a hope.

I make the argument informally with stories, anecdotes, reflections, my favorite historical references, and quotations that I've collected in a lifetime of reading. Since this may be my last book, I have felt free to lift a few sentences or paragraphs from some of my earlier books and from old articles and a few more recent ones—with acknowledgments (below) to editors and publishers. Still, this book's argument is new or, at least, newly imagined. The politics isn't new, but I think I have figured out a new way of describing and defending it.

I have been inspired by two books whose titles include the adjective "liberal" and honor it. The first is *Liberal Socialism* by the Italian socialist and antifascist fighter Carlo Rosselli. Imprisoned by Mussolini in 1927, Rosselli escaped to France, where, with other exiles, he continued the struggle against fascism. He was murdered by Mussolini's thugs in 1937. Two years before that he published his defense of an undogmatic, democratic, and pluralist socialism—most of which had been written while he was in prison. The book was finally translated into English in 1994, edited and with an introduction by Nadia Urbinati.

The second book is *Liberal Nationalism* by the Israeli intellectual and sometime politician Yael Tamir (she was minister of immigration and minister of education in two of Israel's center-left governments—alas, too long ago). Her book was originally a doctoral dissertation written at Oxford; Isaiah Berlin was her academic advisor. The book deals with nationalism across the board, but it is at the same time a defense of Tamir's undogmatic, democratic, and pluralist Zionism.

So the adjective "liberal" belonged first to Rosselli and Tamir. I have tried to make it my own.

I first made the argument about the uses of this adjective in an article in *Dissent* magazine in 2020, mistitled "What It Means to Be Liberal"—it was actually about what it means to be a liberal *something:* a socialist, a nationalist, as in the Rosselli and Tamir books. The noun in these phrases describes the commitment; the adjective tells us about the quality of the commitment.

I am grateful to Michael Kazin, then co-editor of *Dissent,* who read an early version of the piece and asked to publish it. Nancy Rosenblum was my first responder; as soon as she received her copy of the magazine, she sent me an email praising the piece—which was when I began to think about expanding it into a little book. Paul Berman, in a long phone conversation, gave me a list of things that I needed to add or revise, which I sat down and added and revised.

I am also indebted to the editors of the online magazines *Tablet* and *Persuasion,* who have posted short pieces of mine, parts of which I have used again here—on immigration, policing, and shopping from *Tablet* and on the Supreme Court and the risks of political life from *Persuasion.* I took a few lines from an article published long ago in *Dissent* for my riff on "socialism would take too many evenings." Terrorism has been my subject again and again over the years; the discussion here derives, distantly, from my "Terrorism: A Critique of Excuses," published in 1989 in *Problems of International Justice* (Routledge), edited by Steven Luper-foy. In the mid-1990s, I wrote a long essay on the separation of religion and politics in the United States, "Drawing the Line," that was published in the *Utah Law Review* (1999); some revised paragraphs from that essay now appear, with permission from the *ULR,* in chapter 8.

Astrid von Busekist, in our book-length conversation (published in the United States as *Justice Is Steady Work*), forced me to think again about many of the things I've written, including things I had, perhaps conveniently, forgotten. My sister, Judith Walzer Leavitt, urged me to include a chapter on liberal feminists; she then read and criticized my draft, as did her husband, Lewis Leavitt, and my wife, Judith Walzer, my daughters, Sarah Walzer and Rebecca Walzer-Goldfeld, and my granddaughter, Katya Barrett (who provided the most extensive comments). I have had more help with this chapter than with any other, but the version here is my own.

I have written too much over the years, and I may have forgotten and failed to recognize sentences and ideas from my past, so I want to thank all my editors and publishers, especially my colleagues at *Dissent* and the editors of the old *New Republic,* where most of my political pieces have appeared, and all the people at Basic Books and Yale University Press, who have overseen the greater number of my books. I will acknowledge some more particular debts as I go along.

The stories I tell about myself and my political friends and comrades are probably of only limited interest, but they may help to illustrate what it means to live, or work at living, with a liberal qualifier. The one adjective together with the different nouns makes for a particular kind of politics, which I try to write about in its full particularity. It is my own politics, so what follows is in part a personal testament, but since it's not only my own, this is also a celebration of all those men and women, democrats, socialists, nationalists, and so on, whose politics is qualified by the adjective "liberal."

The Struggle for a Decent Politics

.

1
Why the Adjective?

Is liberalism an ism like all the other isms? I think it once was. In the nineteenth century and for some years and in some places in the twentieth, liberalism was an encompassing ideology: free markets, free trade, free speech, open borders, a minimal state, radical individualism, civil liberty, religious toleration, minority rights. But this ideology is now called libertarianism, and most Americans who identify themselves as liberals don't accept it—at least, not all of it. The minimal state and the free market have been replaced among liberals in the United States by different versions of regulation, welfare provision, and (very modest) redistribution; radical individualism has been replaced by greater and lesser (mostly lesser) degrees of mutual aid and communal commitment.

It is worth remembering an older understanding of the word "libertarian"—associated with writers like the Russian revolutionary Peter Kropotkin and groups like the Spanish anarchists of the 1930s. With them the word described a left politics of spontaneous cooperation among free and equal individuals. But radical individualism and equality are rarely seen together in these latter days, and I am not sure they fit together in what we used to call the real world.

Liberalism in Europe today is represented by a few political parties, like the German Free Democrats, that are libertarian in the contemporary sense and therefore right-wing, but also by parties, like the Liberal Democrats in the United Kingdom, that stand uneasily between conservatives and socialists, taking policies and programs from each side without a strong creed of their own. By contrast, US liberalism, as I have already indicated, is our version of social democracy: "New Deal liberalism." It has been fiercely attacked in recent decades as a far-left ideology, which it certainly isn't. Nor is it a strong creed, as we saw when many liberals supposedly committed to it became neoliberals.

The neoliberal program of the 1990s and into the 2000s—economic austerity, deregulation, and reduced provision for welfare—represented a halfway return to the nineteenth-century doctrine. It wasn't fully libertarian, but it was something close, as the success of the Tea Party among Republicans suggests. Tea Party activists described their critique of big government as a defense of liberty against state power, but they made no similar critique of the banks and corporations that represent economic power. As a result, liberty got a less than full-scale defense, while inequality was effectively, and probably intentionally, promoted.

The Democratic version of neoliberalism in the Clinton and Obama years was both a halfway and a halfhearted politics: austerity with a human face, the end, but not entirely, of welfare as we knew it (the highly compromised Affordable Care Act was a partial exception). Democratic politicians pretty much abandoned the commitment of New Deal liberals to the well-being of those at the lower end of the capitalist hierarchy. They watched, and did little to prevent, the steady decline of the unions. In effect, they cut the connections they had once established with the working class and were then unable to deal with the populism and nationalism that their policies helped to provoke. Neoliberalism was never a sustaining or a sustainable creed, and we are likely to see it abandoned by most of its defenders in the years to come. President Joe Biden and his advisors and allies have attempted a full abandonment and a

New Deal restoration but without the success that they promised in 2020.

Liberals are still an identifiable group, and I assume that the readers of this book are members of the group. We may miss out on the oldest understanding of the word, where it describes a life of cultivation and leisure—not the leisure of the idle rich but rather a reflective and slow-paced engagement with the "liberal arts" and with classical learning. A gentleman in the old days, and sometimes a gentlewoman, was not only a rank-holder in the social hierarchy but also and more importantly a person with gentle manners and an inquiring mind. Today, I think, liberals like us are best described in moral rather than political or cultural terms: we are, or we aspire to be, open-minded, generous, and tolerant. We are able to live with ambiguity; we are ready for arguments that we don't feel we have to win. Whatever our ideology, whatever our religion, we are not dogmatic; we are not fanatics. Or, as the actress Lauren Bacall told an interviewer, a liberal is someone who "doesn't have a small mind."

The liberal sensibility that goes along with the morality is almost certainly better represented in literature than in politics. I have learned at least to sense the sensibility and to value it by reading poets like Wisława Szymborska from Poland, Yehuda Amichai from Israel, and three Americans, Philip Levine from Detroit, Philip Schultz from New York, and C. K. Williams from Princeton. There are others, too, but these five especially have taught me something about the generosity, the compassion, the humor, and the gentle irony that go along with the adjective "liberal" but that don't preclude anger and a fierce realism.

Liberal morality is sometimes summed up as "live and let live," but that's not quite right, for we are not relativists. We recognize moral limits; above all, we oppose every kind of bigotry and cruelty.

My teacher and friend Judith Shklar, in a lovely book about the seven deadly sins, argues that we should always "put cruelty first" among the sins we try to avoid (*Ordinary Vices,* 1984). That is a good introduction to liberal morality.

I believe that Democrats and Republicans, and lowercase democrats and republicans, and libertarians and socialists can and should be liberals of this kind. For all these groups, taken at their best, liberal morality comes with the territory. But neither old-fashioned liberalism, nor neoliberalism, nor democratic socialism, nor any comprehensive ideology, is enjoined by liberal morality or liberal sensibility: we all know dogmatic and intolerant democrats and republicans, libertarians and socialists. So what does liberal morality have to do with politics?

This book is an attempt to answer that question—but not in general or universal terms; I don't have an answer for everybody. I mean to write about myself and my political friends and comrades and to tell stories about our common life. How are we, democrats and socialists, connected to a liberal morality? Or, how does a liberal morality shape left politics at home and abroad if and when it does? I will say something about the centrist and rightward versions of this morality, but my first concern is with those on the left—including nationalist, communitarian, feminist, and religious leftists.

Our connection with liberalism has a form very different from that suggested by the noun and the ism. I think of it as an adjectival connection: we are, or we should be, liberal democrats and liberal socialists. I am also a liberal nationalist and internationalist, a liberal communitarian, a liberal feminist, a liberal professor and sometime intellectual, and a liberal Jew. The adjective works in roughly the same way in all these cases, and my aim is to describe its force in each of them. Like all adjectives, "liberal" modifies and complicates the nouns it precedes; it has an effect that is sometimes constraining, sometimes enlivening, sometimes transforming. It determines not who we are but how we are who we are—how we enact our ideological commitments.

In its original meaning, liberalism was a Western ideology, the product of the Enlightenment and the triumph (in literature and philosophy, if not in everyday life) of the emancipated individual—a Western figure. But the adjectives "liberal" and "illiberal" can usefully describe the members of other cultures who use other nouns to name their commitments and who qualify those nouns in a different idiom. I assume that liberal morality and liberal sensibility are universal. They must be, since they are visibly under assault these days around the world—under assault, too, here in the United States.

I will look, chapter by chapter, at the nouns that define my own commitments, and in one chapter my vocation, and then try to describe exactly how the adjective "liberal" qualifies the commitment. My argument, most simply, is that the adjective can't stand by itself as it is commonly made to do (by adding the "ism"); it needs its nouns. But the nouns, the substantive commitments, will never be what they should be without the adjective "liberal."

Without the adjective, democrats, socialists, nationalists, and all the others can be, and often are, monist, dogmatic, intolerant, and repressive. The adjective, as I will try to show, constrains the use of force and makes for pluralism, skepticism, and irony.

2

Liberal Democrats

From the beginning, slavery, racism, misogyny, xenophobia, and class war have shadowed democracy. Democratic politicians have ruled over slaves, women, foreigners, and local proletarians without ever thinking to ask their consent. The first undemocratic democracy in history was Athens, and the Athenian statesman Pericles was probably the first, and certainly the greatest, undemocratic democrat. Nobody's perfect, as they say, but the history of democratic politics suggests a stronger line: everybody is radically imperfect.

The idea is a good one: the people shall rule themselves; governments must rely on the consent of a popular majority formed by free-wheeling debate. But who is counted in determining the majority? Who are the people? In principle, the term is inclusive: all the inhabitants of the city or the state. Self-government is not served if some people govern and other people are governed. That is, however, what goes on in most democracies. The practice is at odds with the principle. In the years since the French Revolution, a long series of political struggles have aimed to bring the two together.

Think of the *demos* at any given moment as the citizens of a city that is subject to repeated invasions by excluded men and women. The invaders are not coming from outside; they already inhabit the city without being its citizens. They are physically but not politically here. The life of the actual citizens is shaped by the exclusions; citizens define themselves with reference to the racial, religious, or ethnic "others" who remain political outsiders. These others are useful servants and menials; the insiders are the masters. It follows that the invaders don't simply enter the city; they transform it. They break, or they begin to break, the established hierarchies. And they won't stop, shouldn't stop, until all of them are inside the political city, part of the *demos,* and all the previously excluded men and women are self-governing citizens. What will that be like? We don't know yet.

This process of progressive inclusion is the working out of democracy itself; no qualifying adjectives are necessary. Sometimes popular empowerment is called radical democracy, but it is better described as democracy itself. The agents of democratization (here in the United States) are workers, women, Blacks, ethnic and religious minorities, and new immigrants fighting for their civil rights. They are supported some of the time by some of the people who already possess civil rights, principled democrats who are called traitors by their fellow insiders. The struggles go on; victories have to be won more than once before they are secure. I suspect that they are never really secure: eternal struggle is the price of democracy. We know today that rights require defense even after those who were excluded are officially citizens. The history of Black struggle in the United States—from the Reconstruction era to the civil rights movement of the 1960s to Black Lives Matter more than half a century later—is proof that battles fought and partially won have to be fought again and again. Racism is America's particular pathology, but there are others, too—the inequalities of class and gender, for example—that require the same politics of repetition, doing the same things over and over.

Still, democracy is an extraordinary project: to create a political order where the greater number of the people, when everyone is counted, actually govern the country. Democracy means majority rule. But what does majority rule mean? What are the rules that govern the rule of the majority? This is where the adjective "liberal" comes into the story.

The conservative writer Brett Stephens recently defined populism as the triumph of democracy over liberalism. I think he meant the triumph of majoritarian democracy over its liberal constraints. Liberal democracy sets limits on majority rule—usually with a constitution that guarantees individual rights and civil liberties, establishes an independent judicial system that can enforce the guarantee, and opens the way for a free press that can defend it. Majorities can only act, or act rightly, within constitutional limits. Like everything else in democratic politics, the limits are disputed both legally and politically. But these disputes are not settled by majority rule but by much more complex processes that work slowly over time, making it difficult to overturn any existing set of rights and liberties.

I do not mean to question the principle of majority rule or the importance of popular agency. The great achievement of democracy is to bring ordinary men and women, you and me, into the decision-making process. We don't only argue among ourselves; we organize social movements and political parties; we join electoral campaigns; and we vote on how things should be or elect representatives who vote on how things should be. But even when we are victorious and our representatives are secure in office, there are limits on the reach of their decisions. Populist demagogues are wrong to claim that once they have won an election, they embody the "will of the People" and can do anything they want. Too often, unhappily, these demagogues, now near-dictators, or Maximal Leaders, really can do anything they want. Still, it is important to insist that there are a lot of things they can't rightly do.

The first thing they want to do is to pass laws that ensure their victory in the next election, which, if they have their way, will be the last meaningful election. They attack the courts and the press; they erode constitutional guarantees; they seize control of the media; they violate the civil rights of opponents and minorities; they reshape the electorate, excluding those who, they claim, are not part of the People; they harass, repress, or arrest the leaders of the opposition—all in the name of majority rule. They are, as Viktor Orbán of Hungary has said, "illiberal democrats."

Democracy was originally understood as the rule of the many, who were assumed to be envious of the wealth of the few and eager to seize it. Populism is the enactment of this understanding, so it is, at least in the beginning, a redistributive politics—although its protagonists have rarely done anything that significantly reduced the wealth of the few. They are, however, generous with state funds, which is the key to their success. They also organize and mobilize the many, offering a special kind of political participation that excludes opposition.

The Maximal Leader is himself (rarely herself) a font of benevolence. As we have seen again and again in Latin America, populists in power spend money on behalf of the people, especially the poorest of the people, who become their most fervent supporters. They hand money out directly, and they expand welfare programs, though usually without recognizing the need to build an economy that can sustain the generosity. Repression and benevolence go hand in hand—until the money runs out, and then the Maximal Leader can rely only on repression.

Populist victories are disasters for everyone on the losing side, defined now as enemies of the People. They are most dangerous for liberal journalists—the everyday voice of opposition, who are often falsely charged with corruption or sedition and locked up. And if the populists, despite all their efforts to ensure victory, were ever to lose an election, that would be a disaster for them—since many liberal democrats—their political foes—believe that their attacks on the constitution and their violations of civil rights were criminal acts. The stakes are very high in this kind of politics. Lose an election, lose power, and go to jail.

There are older ways of enforcing the high stakes of political conflict, ways liberal democrats have come to avoid. In ancient Athens, a politician seen by the people as a threat to democratic rule could be voted into exile (ostracized). In republican Rome, defeat often took a similar form—the ancient world had not heard of Thomas Hobbes's dictum "A change of air is no punishment." Being forced to leave Athens or Rome was considered punishment enough. But Hobbes's view was probably more common in early modern times and probably is today, too. The regicides who fled England in 1660 after the collapse of the Puritan commonwealth did not think that they were being punished; they escaped execution and enjoyed the relative freedom of the American colonies. Today we think of John Locke's years in Holland as an honorable exile—like that of Karl Marx in England after 1848, or that of thousands of political dissidents in the years since. Still, we would not consider exile the proper outcome of a lost election in a democratic state.

In the history of political defeat, death is more likely than exile. Remember King David giving his son Solomon a short list of people who had to be killed to ensure the succession, starting with the old warrior Joab: "Do therefore according to thy wisdom, and let not his hoary head go down to the grave in peace." Imperial politics in ancient Rome was similarly murderous; the assassination of Julius Caesar by men who claimed to defend the republic began a long series of ruthless killings driven by palace intrigue. In the absolute monarchies of early modern Europe, defeated courtiers sent to prison knew that this was only a prelude to execution. Hilary Mantel's novelistic account of the career of Thomas Cromwell is a brilliant portrait of this kind of royal politics. When Cromwell's rivals in the court of Henry VIII succeeded in winning the king's ear, there was no possibility that Cromwell could retire to his country house. He was too dangerous to his courtier enemies; his defeat was not only political but also personal: he had to die.

The liberal constraints on parliamentary politics in eighteenth-century England were a kind of disaster avoidance for everyone involved. Constitutional democracy strengthens the constraints. The aim is to lower the stakes of political conflict. Losing an election leaves you still possessed of all your civil rights—including the right of opposition, which carries with it the hope of victory next time. Rotation in and out of office is a regular feature of liberal democracy. Obviously, no officeholder wants to rotate out of office, but all officeholders live with the risks of rotation. Those risks do not, however, include imprisonment, exile, or death. Lose an election, lose power, and go home.

The expectation of a peaceful transfer of power, without death or prison for the losers, is what made the 2016 chants of "Lock her up!" so shocking. Donald Trump encouraged the chants but didn't make any serious effort to send Hillary Clinton to jail after his victory in the presidential election. He must hope for similar restraint following his own defeat in 2020 (and in any future election). Even after the events of January 6, 2021, when a mob that he incited invaded the Capitol, I still thought that sending him home was the right thing to do—and then working hard to keep him there. Impeachment, if it had worked, would have served the country well; censure, too. But "Lock him up" is not a chant for liberal democrats during or after an election. It is better to say, even in the case of a Donald Trump: "That's not what we do."

The constraints imposed by the adjective "liberal" are understood in exactly this way by Carlo Rosselli in his book *Liberal Socialism.* "Liberal" describes, he writes, "a complex of rules of the game that all the parties in contention commit themselves to respect, rules intended to ensure the peaceful co-existence of citizens . . . ; to restrain competition . . . within tolerable limits; [and] to permit the various parties to succeed to power in turn." So Rosselli's liberal socialism incorporates liberal democracy. For him, as for the democrats he follows, the adjective "liberal" is not only a constraining but also a pluralizing force: it guarantees the existence of "various parties" (more than one) and sustains for each the possibility of success. Liberal socialism, writes Nadia Urbinati in her introduction to the American edition of Rosselli's book, requires "loyalty to a framework that presupposes an antagonistic and pluralistic society."

Karl Marx argued long ago that the final victory of the proletariat in the class struggle would end all forms of social antagonism. There would be only one class of equal citizens: one class, one set of interests, nothing important to argue about. Pluralism might still exist, but this would be a pluralism of architectural styles, literary theories, and sports organizations—definitely not of "various parties" competing for power. Government of the people, taken by Marx and his colleague Friedrich Engels to be necessarily repressive, would be replaced by the "administration of things"—which presumably would set the people free. More likely, they would be treated like things by the appointed administrators—who might well be dominated in turn by an absolute and all-powerful Administrator. That would certainly be an illiberal outcome; the triumph of a liberal communism, if there is such a thing, would look very different. It would look like liberal democracy.

Maximal Leaders are a threat to liberal democracy and, down the road, to democracy itself. But the remedy isn't leaderlessness. In the 1960s and again in the 2020s, some left organizations adopted what they claim is a form of radical democracy: no leaders and no authorized spokesmen. No spokeswomen either, although this version of radicalism is aimed first of all at the Great Man—figures like Charles de Gaulle and Winston Churchill writ small but playing too big a part in the movement. In fact, the absence of leaders does not enhance democracy. Bruce Hartford, a veteran of the 1960s civil rights movement, says what needs to be said: "In real life, 'leaderlessness' simply allows the loudest voices, the most charismatic, the most manipulative, and the most threatening to dominate and intimidate everyone else—with no accountability at all."

Occupy Wall Street in 2011 was a benign example of leaderlessness, with a different set of problems. There wasn't enough time for manipulation or domination. For a heady moment there was egalitarian anonymity (do you remember a single name?). Occupy's critique of inequality—of the 1 percent and the 99 percent—resonated across the country. But the resonance was brief; the moment had no organizational continuation. Five years later, Donald Trump was elected president. His single legislative accomplishment was a tax reform that greatly enriched the 1 percent.

Democratic politics requires a domestic version of nation-building. It requires the creation of oppositional parties and movements that can direct and sustain political activity—with some of them ready to rotate into office if the opportunity arises. Sudden and spontaneous uprisings are not enough. The left, as much as the right, needs accountable leaders who can speak for the others, propose and defend political programs, make decisions, and enforce the discipline necessary for nonviolent marches and demonstrations, which are crucial forms of political opposition.

There is nothing illiberal about a disciplined movement so long as the discipline is self-imposed, a kind of restraint from within, like the restraint of a liberal democracy. The marshals of a march, trained in advance to keep the peace, are the arm of a responsible leadership.

They also express the commitment of the marchers, who are like democratic citizens. They understand that they can't do whatever they want. "Do your own thing!" is not a democratic slogan. A liberal democratic state is designed to prevent state officials from violating the rights of individuals in the name of majority rule. A liberal democratic movement is designed to prevent militants from violating the rights of their fellow citizens: harassing bystanders, breaking windows, burning cars, looting stores, in the name of revolution. The first restraint prevents tyranny, the second anarchy. (There is also a peaceful and libertarian version of anarchy, but that version hasn't been evident when movement discipline breaks down.)

Discipline is also necessary for civil disobedience, which is the right way to break the law in a democratic society. In North Carolina in 1960, the Black students sitting in and refusing to leave Woolworth's segregated lunch counters said that their nonviolence was entirely pragmatic. It wasn't religiously motivated, they explained, like that of the Black preachers, who would be nonviolent anywhere. Actually, both piety and pragmatism were in play among the students. They respected the religious leaders of their communities, although they often argued with them. And being politically smart, they recognized the coercive power of the (White) authorities. Respect and prudence together contributed to the extraordinary self-discipline and solidarity of the early civil rights movement.

But civility in the form of nonviolence is also mandated by a respect for democratically enacted laws. No doubt, the *demos* isn't as inclusive as it should be, and popular majorities often get things wrong. Nonviolent civil disobedience signals opposition only to the wrongs, not to the democratic process itself or to the values that the process embodies. Along with the preachers, the students sitting in were appealing to the religious idea that all human beings are created in God's image; they were also appealing to what they hoped were the deepest political commitments of their fellow citizens.

Responsible leaders and the discipline of nonviolence work, much like pluralism and rotation in office, to lower the stakes of political conflict. Student leaders in the early civil rights movement were first among equals; they answered to their fellows and to their communities; they weren't looking for a fight-to-the-death politics. Political activists like those young people in the South, or like most of the men and women fighting for social justice or gender equality or labor rights anywhere in the country, begin by announcing to their opponents: "We are nonviolent, so you must be, too." It often doesn't work, as the 1968 police riot in Chicago and many incidents in civil rights and union history amply demonstrate. But the commitment is important; it is morally right and politically reassuring. The movements aim at winning; they aim at social transformation—and that is certain to frighten not only right-wing opponents but also ordinary citizens who are accustomed to the way things are and worried by new ideas. Movement activists should never give them reason to be frightened for their lives or their property. By property I mean their small-holdings; the riches of the rich may rightly be at risk.

What if the struggle goes on and on without success? The police response is brutal, the activists don't win. Or, like the civil rights activists of the 1960s, they win something, but far less than they hoped for. "We overcame," they might say, "but not overall." The structures and practices of American racism remain, not wholly but substantially, intact. Disproportionate numbers of Blacks continue to live in poverty, endure ill health and unemployment, and die at the hands of the police. As a consequence, periodically, always suddenly, demonstrations are replaced by riots: windows are smashed, shops looted, police cars burned. Tobi Haslett has written a powerful, passionate, and romantic essay (in the magazine *n+1*) celebrating the riots that followed the police murder of George Floyd in 2020. The riots were for him a vision of revolutionary action that "propelled and made fiercely possible" the extraordinary mass protests across America that summer—the peaceful protests that people like me happily joined. "The riots worked," Haslett writes; "the beast groaned."

But in the cities where the riots were like actual insurrections (Minneapolis, Portland, Seattle), more people were frightened and turned away than moved to join the struggle. Violence of the sort welcomed by Haslett doesn't work in a democratic society, however flawed the democracy. What the militants burn, they can't replace; liberated areas turn into criminal hangouts; ordinary activists go home. Still, there might be a dialectical relation between riot and protest or, better, a division of labor: you break windows; I demonstrate and march, and between us we will change the world (or the city). I am doubtful. Riots haven't yet opened the way to revolution or to any transformative politics. They probably feed the counterrevolution, the forces that claim to represent law and order. Real change requires that a mobilization of the moment turn itself into a disciplined movement capable of acting day after day. That won't bring revolution either, but things may move slowly forward—as in Antonio Gramsci's "war of position," whose militants aim at cultural as well as political change and work steadily, with a long horizon. "In politics," Gramsci writes, "the war of position, once won, is decisive definitively." But that is not a promise.

A wide-open competition for power, with much at stake but not everything; an ongoing struggle for social change, transformative but not revolutionary—these are crucial features of liberal democracy but not the whole story. The pluralizing effects of the adjective "liberal" reach into every corner of the democratic state. They make for a wonderfully lively civil society, densely and diversely populated. Every possible kind of association is represented, all of them standardly described as voluntary associations—although liberal communitarians, who admire the pluralism, have a more nuanced view of the voluntarism (as I will argue later on).

Civil society is where men and women choose their friends, colleagues, comrades, and fellows. The civil society of a liberal democracy includes not only political parties and social movements but also associations for religious worship and schooling; for mutual aid and cultural expression; for communal defense and ethnic or racial advancement; for charitable work; for daycare and preschool programs and adult education. There are also associations that foster common interests and hobbies—collecting (almost anything), playing games in real and surreal spaces, hiking, reading books together—and still others that advance causes that don't quite rise to the movement level: the prevention of cruelty to animals; vegetarianism and veganism; neighborhood safety and beautification; help for people in trouble after a fire or hurricane; the promotion of this or that version of a healthy life. The causes and purposes multiply; the groups grow and decline, come and go, as they compete for attention, influence, members, and money. People organize services, meetings, classes, celebrations; hold rallies; provide summer camps, trips abroad, and ocean cruises (with attendant lecturers); launch fund-raising campaigns; and publish magazines and newsletters for members. They are online and even, still, in the streets, knocking on doors.

All this is the common life of a liberal democracy. Groups like these can exist and activities like these can go on in illiberal and undemocratic societies. But there they are likely to be taken in hand by the one-party state or the Maximal Leader and his followers. The multitude of groups will be pared down, the activities controlled, the publications censored. Nothing quite like that happens here in the United States, although we have had moments of state-organized repression. Ours is a seriously imperfect liberal democracy, where radical inequality makes it difficult for many Americans to participate fully in the activities of civil society. But for those who are engaged and active, the vitality of associational life is evident; indeed, it is exhausting—there are too many demands on their time and energy.

What the adjective "liberal" most importantly guarantees is the freedom, the openness, of civil society. A simple story will illustrate how this works. In the 1970s, I was a member of a small philosophical discussion group. In order to obtain (very little) financial support from our universities, we gave the group a name, SELF, the Society for Ethical and Legal Philosophy. Among ourselves, pretentiously, we were the Society for the Elimination of Lousy Philosophy. Our program, insofar as we had one, was to bring philosophy to bear on current political and social issues. Our members were mostly liberals and leftists. But we never had to register with the authorities; no government agency invited any of us to report on each other. Our university funding was for travel (we alternated between two cities for our meetings), but no university official asked where we were going. After a few years of discussion, we decided to found a magazine where we, and others like us, could argue about questions of immediate relevance: war, affirmative action, inequality, justice in taxation, and many others. We had little trouble finding support for publication (a few of our members were philosophical notables); none of the supporters ever interfered with the contents of the magazine. We chose an editor, and he, together with a few advisors from SELF, decided which articles to print and which to reject. We looked for readers in competition with a very large number of other academic and political magazines.

In those same years, dissident philosophers in Eastern Europe and the Soviet Union were also meeting and writing and trying to publish what they wrote. But they met in secret, quietly, in each other's living rooms. They had to trust each other, although that was hard since there were often informers in their midst. The authorities took an interest; the meetings were dangerous. What these philosophers wrote was *samizdat* ("self-published"), and although they imagined themselves to be with friends and comrades, writing was a lonely business. The Russian dissident Vladimir Bukovsky defined *samizdat* this way: "I write it myself, I edit it myself, I censor it myself, I publish it myself, I distribute it myself, and I spend time in prison for it myself." (Bukovsky spent twelve years in psychiatric prisons and labor camps.) The dissident philosophers longed for a liberal democracy like ours, where "self" could have a different meaning. Writing philosophy underground may be more exciting, even more meaningful, than writing in the open, freely. Certainly, the stakes are higher. But most philosophers would choose the openness that the adjective "liberal" guarantees.

How open should civil society be, however? That is a perennial question. Is there space available in a liberal democracy for antidemocratic parties and movements to organize and agitate? Does the free speech that is constitutionally guaranteed include hate speech? I won't attempt a closely argued answer to these questions; liberal democrats are ready defenders of all our civil liberties—free speech, free press, and free association. But I want to worry a bit about whether the absolutist defense of these liberties is required by the adjective "liberal." That is the common view, but surely "absolute" and "liberal" are words that sit uneasily together. Senator Barry Goldwater's claim that "extremism in defense of liberty is no vice" does not sound like the beginning of a liberal argument.

Consider the famous case of the neo-Nazi march planned for Skokie, Illinois, in 1978. Among the inhabitants of Skokie, a suburb of Chicago, were a large number of Holocaust survivors—that is why the neo-Nazis wanted to march there. They wanted the survivors to remember what Nazism was and to fear its return. (I am not sympathetic to critics of the proposed march who said that it would be "hurtful" to the survivors; it was much more than that: it was a political and indeed a physical challenge to their existence.) The American Civil Liberties Union defended the planned march against all efforts to stop it by city officials, who invoked local ordinances against disorder and riot. Similar ordinances had been used in the South in the 1960s to prevent civil rights marches. Today, the ACLU boasts of its fierce defense of free speech. It won the legal case in Skokie, but the march, as things turned out, was never held. I can see the legal argument—that the law should be the same for African Americans defending equality and for Nazis defending genocide. But I think that the adjective "liberal" precludes any moral equivalence between the two groups or between the meaning of their marches—and if they are not morally similar (or even close), do they really have to be treated in the same way? It might have been better if the ACLU had defended the civil rights marchers and declined to defend the neo-Nazis. Just a touch of skepticism about civil liberties absolutism, an acknowledgment of possible (not many) exceptions, would serve the cause of liberal democracy.

But we do want people marching—some people, some of the time. I am not sure that what we called participatory democracy in the 1960s is an example of liberal democracy. In the political movements of those years democracy often amounted to the rule of the participants, which meant in practice the rule of the young militants who had time for all the meetings. I will come back to this issue when I discuss the civic republicanism favored by some communitarian theorists. It is enough to say here that political and social movements like the civil rights and antiwar movements of the 1960s need the militants, need their commitment and the hours they spend, and may have to accept their dominance. But the democratic government of cities and states is not a movement.

Liberal democracy enables citizen activism, and we liberals hope to see a lot of people arguing, organizing, demonstrating, and voting. But liberal democracy also allows and tolerates different degrees of activity and inactivity. Everyone must be able to join the political and electoral contests, but there must also be room for people who hold back because they aren't interested in politics, and room also for people with overriding family and work obligations, and for people who come and go, intermittent participants, who watch from the sidelines and kibbitz. Liberal democrats will recognize what Irving Howe, my teacher at Brandeis University and my political mentor, called "a right not to participate"—which may be a close cousin to another right defended back in the 1880s by Paul Lafargue, Marx's son-in-law: the right to be lazy.

What holds activists and non-activists together? I described civil society in a liberal democracy as a pluralist world of (mostly) voluntary associations, which people join and leave freely. Now I have described democratic politics as a world of active and inactive citizens, full-time, part-time, and no-time participants. So who constitutes the *demos* — the "people," the collective "self" of self-determination? It might appear that the adjective "liberal" disassembles the *demos.* There may be some truth to that idea: liberal democrats may be less responsive to the demands of a common identity, less amenable to collective discipline, and more resistant to discipline imposed without their agreement. But there is no reason to think that they won't be tax-paying, law-abiding, and (at least sometimes) politically engaged citizens. Citizenship itself is what holds them together; they are equal members of the political community, and they recognize themselves and each other as equal members. They accept that all have a right to participate in decision-making, whether they participate or not, and that all have to live with the consequences of the decisions made. There are common goods and common bads produced by the practice of self-government. The citizens are united in their desire to have the goods and avoid the bads. We are all in the same boat.

Apart from these common desires, the people in the boat share a civil religion—religion-lite according to some, but real enough, with rituals, holidays, and authoritative texts: the naturalization process, the oaths of office, the national anthem, the Pledge of Allegiance, the Fourth of July, Memorial Day, the Declaration of Independence, and the Constitution. No doubt, this religion lacks the intensity of religions that have existed for thousands of years; it is a religion with a creed, perhaps, but without a theology. Still, it has its moments.

Citizenship with its attendant interests and rituals can make for a strong political fellowship; it may be even more important in sustaining a democratic government. In the political crisis that culminated on January 6, 2021, the country was bitterly divided; the political class was, too. But the civil service held firm for constitutional democracy. The far-right and neofascist rioters had no support from the deep state (the national security agencies). And what was more of a surprise to many of us on the left, they also had no support from what might be called the "ground-level state"—the range of civil servants from judges and state officials to ordinary citizens counting the ballots. All of them seem to have been motivated by something like what Jürgen Habermas called "constitutional patriotism."

Still, in the difficult months from the November 2020 election to the invasion of the Capitol, a lot of Americans who considered themselves patriots thought that all those civil servants were traitors. The Washington mob claimed to be defending the real America, which they took to be a White Christian nation. They were illiberal nationalists and perhaps also illiberal communitarians—and they were, I believe, terribly wrong about America. But we should stop for a moment to ask the questions their politics poses. Is it possible to sustain a society like ours through good times and bad without a singular, anti-pluralist understanding of what America means? Maybe the pronoun "we" has to refer to people with a shared history, culture, and religion in addition to or prior to their shared material interests and civic identity. Maybe the Constitution and the sense of living in the same boat aren't enough without the supposed emotional bond of racial and religious singularity.

A brief poem by Walt Whitman suggests otherwise (Sam Beer, my Harvard protector, told me to read this poem):

> One's-Self I sing, a simple separate person,
> Yet utter the word Democratic, the word En-Masse.
>
> Of physiology from top to toe I sing,
> . . .
> The Female equally with the Male I sing.
>
> Of Life immense in passion, pulse, and power,
> Cheerful, for freest action form'd under the laws divine,
> The Modern Man I sing.

Whitman, the modern man, is a "simple separate person," but at the same time he is united with the democratic others, men and women, en masse, all together. His is a multitudinous America, radically diverse, full of contradictions, "immense in passion, pulse, and power," but not necessarily divided or, if divided, not bitterly so. I hear America singing, he wrote in another poem, and he thought that sometimes, at least, "the varied carols I hear" were also "strong melodious songs."

Nationalists and communitarians have their own answers to the question "What holds us together?" Some of them agree with the Trumpian rioters at least this far: that a common life and a common good depend on the kind of fervor that we associate with the old religions—heightened feelings of membership and a wariness of "others." But what happened on January 6 suggests that political emotions can be as divisive as political interests, maybe more so. Nationalism in the United States, as I will argue later, is more dividing than unifying, more often directed against fellow citizens than against foreign countries. And communitarians often write as if they are living in another, more homogenous country, not Whitman's America or ours.

I hope that liberal democrats will stick with the idea that citizenship, material interest, and our modest civil religion (together with an appreciation for the varied carols we hear) are the best unifiers of a highly diverse political society like ours—and will embrace the social and economic policies that follow from that idea. Many of the Americans who supported Donald Trump and sympathized with the Capitol rioters had lost what political scientists call their "sense of efficacy"; they were angry, resentful, dysfunctional citizens, and their political disconnection was intensified by a new economic vulnerability and a not unreasonable belief that the country's rulers had given up on them. They had been left behind; they were no longer part of Whitman's complex American melody. I don't know how to bring them back, but one way to begin—just that: to begin—is to work for a politics of inclusion, where everyone's material interests are of equal concern.

Even if democratic citizenship and constitutional patriotism are only partial remedies to our divisions, they are necessary remedies. Their force depends in significant ways on the success of democratic education, which is centrally concerned with the reproduction of citizens and which ought to promote a sense of democratic commitment of each citizen to all the others. But public education in its liberal version will also create independent minds and enable social criticism, which some people, illiberal democrats, take to be an affront to the unity of the people. In the educational world today there are many fiercely illiberal voices addressing issues, necessary issues, of race and racism. We have populist politicians on the right trying to rule out any criticism of American institutions and militants on the left vilifying anyone who fails to get the criticism exactly right—which just shows how important our schools are.

Virtually all citizens of the United States spent years in school when they were children, and they should have taken courses in American government, history, and literature. The first two of these were required courses in my high school for students in both the academic and the vocational tracks. Democracy would seem to require the education of all the boys and girls who will one day shape its political life. Although democratic Athens had no public schools, Aristotle believed them to be essential: "The system of education in a state must be one and the same for all, and the provision of this system must be a matter of public action." Today, when systems of this sort are common in democratic states, one of the first things that populists and nationalists do when they come to power is to seize control of the schools. They rewrite the textbooks to reflect their authoritarian ideology; they recruit ideologically committed teachers and purge those with dissident opinions; they aim at political indoctrination and at an exclusionary patriotism. By contrast, there is a close connection between liberal democracy and liberal education—a connection first worked out by John Dewey, who was America's philosopher much the way Aristotle was Athens's.

Dewey's program for a "progressive" education suited to a democratic culture was directed against all the rigidities of traditional schooling: authoritarian teachers, tight classroom discipline, and rote learning. (I remember a high school civics teacher who, having brought us too quickly through the textbook on constitutional democracy, with two weeks left in the semester, ordered us to memorize the glossary of terms.) Dewey and his followers thought that a more cooperative educational process, where students learned at their own pace, participated in curricular decision-making, and were encouraged to think critically, was the right preparation for democratic citizenship. Some skeptics argued that too much participation by children, who didn't yet know very much, led to less learning of basic subjects like reading and arithmetic. Teachers had to take charge, they argued. Certainly, the inequality of teachers and students is not inconsistent with the future equality of citizens. But the authority of the teachers has to be genuinely helpful to each of the very different boys and girls in the class—and that requires a democratic engagement with all of them. That was Dewey's main point. His schools would produce young adults with inquiring minds. They might not be nationalists or communitarians, but they would be good constitutional patriots.

The existence of millions of fellow citizens who believe in "alternative facts" and conspiracy theories strongly suggests that our schools aren't producing enough science-savvy and tough-minded realists. What seems most necessary right now is an enhanced education in what might be called critical empiricism: what facts are, how science works, what "truth" means, and how to detect lies. We need to encourage teachers to engage with their students on these issues in everything they teach, from biology and physics to history and English. This is probably more urgent than teaching about diversity, or identity, or even critical race theory (a good subject for a college course). We should, of course, provide our schools with textbooks that tell the truth about slavery, about the failure of Reconstruction and the long history of racist discrimination, about anti-immigrant nativism, and about the internment of Japanese Americans during World War II—but also about the remarkable persistence of democratic institutions in the United States for two and a half centuries. Teachers need to tell the truth, all of it, and teach it in a way that also teaches truth-telling.

A Rousseauian version of participatory democracy would replace professional teachers with supposedly wise elderly citizens, who are said to embody the values of the community—and, similarly, it would replace professional police with neighborhood committees, and professional politicians with direct democracy, the rule of everyone. I will leave the questions of governance and policing to the chapter on communitarianism and argue here in defense of professionalism in education. The key slogan of the liberal and democratic revolutions of the eighteenth and nineteenth centuries was "careers open to talents." Open careers are a challenge to caste societies, where children inherit the status and work (or leisure) of their parents. But they are also incompatible with a society where, as Rousseau says, the citizens do everything for themselves. Careers can be open to talents only if there are careers to which the talented can aspire, jobs they can hope to do. We all want to be served by competent people, just as parents want their children taught by teachers who know a lot about the subjects they teach and about the psychology of the boys and girls in their classroom. It is no less important that competent people be able to find work—offices, professions, and responsibilities—that matches their competence. People who want to teach should be able to work at making themselves good professional teachers. Perhaps this is "the pursuit of happiness."

The high school I attended many years ago was a consolidated school; the students came from middle-class and working-class neighborhoods; the school was ethnically diverse, but all White. The teachers were also all White, and all of them were committed to the conventions of the Cold War. But they were also professionals. In the early 1950s, the Pennsylvania State Legislature passed a law to encourage driver-training courses in high schools: the state would provide a free car to any high school that set up a course. In the town where I lived, the school board thought this an example of "creeping socialism," rejected the offer, and refused to teach us how to drive. I circulated a petition calling on the board to reverse its decision. The school's history teacher called me in and asked me where my parents came from (a clear example of what is today called micro-aggression). I think she believed that they must be Russian communists. New York and Connecticut, I told her. I don't remember her response, but at the end of the year, she graded me fairly in World History. She was a bigoted woman but also a professional teacher. The community elders would probably have treated me worse.

Professional teachers have to be paid well for the work they do. In the United States, they are notoriously underpaid, except in a few cities where they have formed powerful unions. They are also under-respected, which is very strange given the importance of the production and reproduction of the democratic ethos—a project that is in large part their responsibility (the responsibility of all the rest of us, too). The democratic ethos, however, doesn't have sufficient market value, and that is what determines how much people earn and how much they are respected in a capitalist society—even when capitalism is supposed to be, what it can never entirely be, democratic. These are questions of special interest to socialists.

Liberal democrats will defend a state where power is constrained, where the common life is pluralist and inclusive, where the right of opposition is protected, where teachers make sure that the curiosity of children is cultivated rather than repressed, and where every man and woman is a political agent, able to join any and all meetings and movements and free to stay home—the equal of all the others. Socialists are committed to a more radical egalitarianism, which reaches from democratic politics across society and economy—and which needs to be qualified in many of the same ways by the adjective "liberal."

3

Liberal Socialists

"Liberal," a strong adjective, constrains not only populist dema-gogues who win elections but also our favorite leftists if and when they win. Looking back, we liberal democrats, and liberal socialists, too, would have had to question President Franklin D. Roosevelt's court-packing scheme of 1937. That example of populism from the left is similar to Donald Trump's effort, eighty years later, to fill the courts with right-wing judges. The claim in both cases is that electoral vic-tory and ideological commitment override judicial impartiality, which in any case is only impartial in pretense. Yes, judges are ideologically as well as legally driven. Judicial decision-making is in part, probably in large part, a political process. That is why liberal democrats and social-ists should argue for judicial deference to the executive and legislative branches—whose members are elected and politically accountable. In cases involving human rights, civil liberty, and the democratic process, however, we want activist judges defending the liberal constraints.

As I write, we have a Supreme Court that gets these things exactly wrong: rejecting efforts by Congress and the White House to move the country toward greater equality (actually, toward less inequality) while refusing to interfere with right-wing attempts to undermine democratic elections. Judicial professionals should recognize the dif-ference between constitutionally guaranteed freedom and democracy, which is their province, and the democratic shaping of the economic order, the task of elected officials.

Judicial professionalism sometimes works—as we saw when judges appointed by presidents from both parties rejected many, though not enough, of Donald Trump's executive orders. But partisan judges may sometimes require partisan correction. FDR schemed to pack the Court in the years of the Great Depression, a time, it might reasonably have been argued, of economic and political emergency. He was facing deeply entrenched corporate resistance to measures he thought economically and socially necessary. Here is an issue that liberal democrats and socialists regularly confront—and the confrontation is never easy (hence the twists and turns of my own argument). What uses of political power are justified in sustaining democracy, dealing with economic crises, moving the country toward social justice, creating an egalitarian society?

Critics say that the liberal left doesn't do well when the going is tough, when politics is tense and opposition fierce. What is necessary then is a strong leader (or a vanguard party) who can break through the barriers of human rights and civil liberty. Commonly on the right and sometimes, as we will see, on the left, writers and politicians invoke the "state of exception" to justify authoritarian measures. FDR's court-packing scheme, which would have required congressional agreement, is a relatively mild example. Two of the most dramatic authoritarian moments in US history involve presidents whom we might otherwise think of as liberal democrats. Abraham Lincoln suspended habeus corpus in the border states during the Civil War, and Roosevelt, during the Second World War, approved the removal of Japanese Americans from the West Coast and their internment in concentration camps—decisions that could never be qualified by the adjective "liberal."

Strong leadership in a crisis is not ruled out by either liberal democrats or liberal socialists. Indeed, libertarian writers, arguing mostly from the right, insist that democrats and socialists are authoritarian by nature: too willing to use the power of the state. Suspending habeus corpus and interning fellow citizens, libertarians would say, are notorious examples that draw attention away from all the more mundane cases of illegitimate coercion. I am writing this in the months of the Covid-19 pandemic when states and cities in the United States, chiefly those with Democratic governors and mayors, mandated vaccinations for state employees and mask wearing and social distancing for everyone—and were challenged in the name of individual liberty. Banning large meetings in enclosed spaces was called socialist regimentation. Conservative judges actually provided some libertarian relief, although the mandates seem to me consistent with the commitment of any government, certainly any democratic or socialist government, to public health and safety. The mandates prohibited self-injury, which I suppose is a natural right, but they also served to prevent injury to others.

What the adjective "liberal" requires is that any coercive executive action be subject to congressional and judicial review and, down the road, to the political test of a free election. Leaders at every level have to be kept politically accountable. Most likely, that will be the chief political lesson of the 2020 pandemic, not the need for a strong leader who can break all the rules, but rather the need for review and accountability when the leader in place is incompetent.

Of course, review and accountability don't necessarily work the way we want them to. The Japanese American internment was reviewed by the Supreme Court, as it should have been, and then allowed by the justices (with notable dissents by Owen Roberts, Frank Murphy, and Robert Jackson: remember the names). In wartime and in civil emergencies generally, the country needs not only a court but a brave court. Any constitutional regime that requires the constraint of power also requires its legislators and judges to act with courage in crises.

But accountability can also take electoral forms. FDR, for example, had to face an election in 1944 in the midst of the war. During the campaign he wasn't criticized for the violation of the rights of Japanese American citizens, but he could have been had his Republican opponent been a better liberal democrat. Winston Churchill, who led Britain through its most desperate hours, sometimes by imposing desperate measures, faced an election in 1945 while the war in Asia was still being fought—and lost the election. I have always considered that one of the great moments in the history of democratic politics. Imagine Joseph Stalin's surprise when Churchill was abruptly replaced at the Potsdam Conference, where the world's leaders were busily designing the postwar world. Churchill's defeat was also a victory for the modest and rather undistinguished (but very effective) leader of the British Labor Party—a good liberal socialist.

An old doctrine of leftist militants is that a liberal socialist like Clement Atlee will never measure up to the requirements of political and economic transformation. The militants don't argue that democrats and socialists are too ready to use coercion, as libertarians claim, but rather that they aren't ready enough to make the exceptions that exceptional moments demand. On this view, Lincoln's suspension of habeus corpus served the cause of abolition, and Roosevelt's internment of Japanese Americans was politically, if not militarily, necessary to the success of an antifascist war. Revolution is itself a war, these militants argue, and the overthrow of capitalism will require a period of dictatorship or, at least, a temporary suspension of civil liberties—a democratic dictatorship of the proletariat or, more likely, an undemocratic dictatorship of the vanguard of the proletariat. Liberal ideas of constraint and accountability have no place in their revolution. Elected assemblies will have to be suspended, their members sent home. Courts defending civil liberties will have to be either repressed or packed with judges who will do as they are told.

Unlike populist rulers, the socialist vanguard does not claim to represent the people or even the working class as it is, but rather the people and the working class as they should be—and will be at the end of the march that the vanguard is leading. The Czech novelist Milan Kundera described the "grand march" to socialism as the classic form of leftist kitsch. But the march is first of all the ideology of the vanguard, whose dictatorship is justified by its certain knowledge of where the march is going. The destination justifies the harsh discipline that is required to get there.

The vanguard generation must endure that discipline for the sake of the generations to come. Hayim Greenberg, a brilliant writer who edited *The Jewish Frontier* years ago and was both a liberal socialist and a liberal nationalist, provides a memorable answer to that argument. He cites what may be its original version—the biblical story of the Israelite exodus from Egypt, in the course of which God decides that the slave generation must die in the wilderness. Only those who don't remember Pharaoh, who are free men and women, can enter the Promised Land. In the future, Greenberg writes, socialists "will be more modest and too skeptical to believe in some Canaan for the sake of which it is permissible to sacrifice an entire generation . . . the happiness of no future generation is worth the sacrifice of present-day sinners." Or, in Greenberg's italics, *"there are no transitional generations in history."* Every generation is an end in itself—which I would translate into a four-word maxim: "No socialism without me!"

Liberal socialists don't necessarily deny that the final overthrow of capitalism would require harsh disciplinary measures. If you believe in finality, then you can't allow "various parties to succeed to power in turn"—since some of them might try to slow down the march, or turn it back, or advance in a different direction. The vanguard can't allow itself to be challenged or replaced. But the repression necessary to avoid replacement, to prevent political opponents from succeeding to power, is incompatible with the socialism that we liberal socialists want. It is also incompatible with the way we mean to march on the way to socialism. We know that we will encounter "conflicts and contradictions," as Greenberg writes, which we will have to resolve as political equals through a democratic process. Dissidents will not be killed or sent to concentration camps—another example of how the adjective "liberal" reduces the risks of political conflict.

Another kind of repression is common to versions of illiberal socialism: the repression required to sustain a regime of radical egalitarianism, the state as a Procrustean bed. Inequality is a constant, and constantly renewed, feature of every human society. Powerful families and ruling classes naturally reproduce themselves, but even if we imagine an original equality, it will not be sustained. Distribute money equally on a Sunday, and it will be unequally redistributed a week later. Individual intelligence, strength, wit, energy, popularity, and luck all make for unequal standing in economy and society. Only the coercive power of the state, applied consistently and in the most detailed way, can keep things even. I doubt that any such use of power has ever been approved democratically, nor has any nondemocratic regime sustained it for long. The lawmakers of ancient Israel intended all purchases and exchanges of land to be annulled every fifty years (in the Jubilee year) and all families returned to their original holdings, which were assumed to have been equal. But they said nothing about how the return was to be enforced, nor were any of the biblical regimes capable of enforcing it. Almost certainly, the return never happened.

In our own time, we have seen fake versions of this kind of egalitarianism—as when everyone in Mao's China (so it seemed) suddenly began wearing the same simple quasi-uniform. But this equality in appearance masked the great inequalities of power and even of wealth in communist China. Much more disturbing are the efforts to achieve equality by killing off or repressing members of an old privileged class—as happened to the kulaks in Stalin's Russia, to "bourgeois elements" during the Chinese Cultural Revolution, and to educated and professional men and women in Khmer Rouge Cambodia. These are instances of an old and certainly illiberal leftism—parodied long ago by Shakespeare in his portrayal of Jack Cade, a fifteenth-century populist, pointing to a cleric and addressing a crowd: "Away with him! Away with him. He speaks Latin."

Men and women characterized by the adjective "liberal" condemn brutal repression and mass murder. But so does (almost) everyone else, though sometimes only after the fact. Critics argue that "liberals" also oppose any root and branch attack on the old order and its inequalities. The adjective, they say, really means "not radical," unable or unwilling to imagine a better society, complacent about this one. This was a common criticism of American liberalism in the early years of the Cold War. In 1950, in *The Liberal Imagination,* Lionel Trilling accused contemporary liberals of living "in an aura of self-congratulation." A few years later, he fell under the aura himself: "In many civilizations there comes a point at which wealth shows a tendency to submit itself, in some degree, to the rule of mind and imagination. . . . In America the signs of this submission have for some time been visible. . . . Intellect has associated itself with power, perhaps as never before in history, and is now conceded to be itself a kind of power." Exactly what sort of power Trilling thought liberal intellectuals like himself were exercising is unclear; it certainly wasn't a transformative power.

But I don't think that the adjective "liberal" necessarily pushes the nouns that it modifies in the direction of complacency and compromise. In the cases relevant here, it is indeed the noun that carries the radicalism and requires those it describes to imagine what Leon Trotsky called "a world more attractive." Democrats are radically opposed to all tyrannical, hierarchical, and oligarchic regimes; they imagine a world of self-governing citizens. Socialists are radically opposed to capitalism, laissez-faire economics, and libertarian politics and to the oppression these three together produce; they imagine a more egalitarian society. Nationalists are radically opposed to imperialism and colonial rule; they imagine an international society of free nations. Communitarians are radically critical of a society of self-regarding individuals; they imagine the warmth of communal mutuality. Feminists are radically critical of the subordination of women in the family, the economy, and the state; they imagine a society marked by gender equality. I will leave aside for now religious groups, where the adjective "liberal" may well mean "not radical" (at least some of the time). Politically it clearly doesn't have that meaning. It means not despotic, not repressive, not cruel—constrained by individual rights. It also means not totalizing, not exclusive, not singular—open to plurality and difference. It points us toward necessary political battles about the quality and character of democracy, socialism, and all the other doctrines and causes—battles that we liberals don't always win.

I suppose there are people who believe that a politics that isn't totalizing and cruel isn't radical or radical enough. But that view doesn't seem plausible to me. The negative injunctions of the adjective "liberal" do affect the kind and quality of socialist egalitarianism, but they don't diminish its opposition to capitalist hierarchy. I will come to the arguments about equality a little later; they are obviously central to the socialist vision. But arguments about authority and the use and misuse of power are central to socialist history.

The adjective "liberal" means that a socialist society can be achieved only with the consent of the people as they are here and now with all their differences of character, belief, and ability, and it must be fought for democratically. The struggle has already been long, and there have been and will be compromises along the way with opponents whose rights we have to respect. Two steps forward, one step back is better than three steps forward over the bodies of our opponents.

There have been too many murdered bodies. The adjective "liberal" is a reminder of the cruelties of the illiberal left. In the course of the twentieth century, regimes calling themselves socialist (and claiming to be marching toward communism) proved to be as murderous as regimes of the right. Liberal socialists today must acknowledge the past, memorialize the victims, and set themselves against any return of authoritarian or totalitarian politics. As we oppose state repression and state terror, we must defend "bourgeois civil liberty"—even while insisting that the adjective "bourgeois" describes only the class origin of civil liberty and does not deny its universal value. Nor are we required to extend the benefits of civil liberty to groups actively and forcefully trying, in the name of vanguard socialism or ultra-nationalism, or any other ideology, to destroy liberal democracy. We liberal democrats and liberal socialists alike learned from the history of the Weimar Republic that the adjective "liberal" has to be consistent with collective self-defense.

Over many years, I wrote for and helped to edit a magazine called *Dissent,* the political home of writers and readers committed to liberal socialism. Most of the time we called ourselves democratic socialists or social democrats, but the adjective "liberal" shaped our politics in critically important ways. The founders of *Dissent* were ex-Trotskyists who had become uncomfortable with the dogmatism and intolerance of sectarian politics. The sect is perhaps the ur-model of an illiberal political organization. Its members respond to political defeat or long-term marginality by intensifying their conviction and confirming to each other the absolute rightness of their ideology and the righteousness of their commitment. The early *Dissent*-niks opted for a wider horizon, a more pluralist politics, and a touch of skepticism about the endpoint of the long march. Irving Howe, one of the founders, liked to tell an old Jewish joke about endings. In an East European shtetl, a man was chosen to sit outside the entrance to the town and watch for the Messiah so the inhabitants would have some warning of his long-awaited coming. A friend asked him, "What kind of a job is that?" "It doesn't pay very well," he answered, "but it is steady work." Liberal socialism is steady work.

The *Dissent*-niks were independent leftists, hostile to Stalinism at a time when many leftists were still defending the Soviet regime, denying its crimes, or apologizing for them in the name of historical necessity and the future triumph of the working class. *Dissent*'s editors were dissidents on the left who sometimes found themselves in an awkward alliance with liberal cold warriors. But when some of the cold warriors embraced McCarthyism (and became, one might say, neoliberal cold warriors), the *Dissent*-niks rallied to the cause of bourgeois civil liberty and defended the rights of communist teachers, actors, and writers. The shock of Stalinism was the most important cause of their liberal commitment. McCarthyism provided an occasion to display it.

The war in Vietnam posed difficult questions for the liberal socialists of *Dissent*. The magazine's founders knew the names of every Trotskyist militant, every independent leftist, who had been murdered by the Vietnamese communists. They foresaw the cruelty that would come (that did come) with the victory of the Vietcong and its North Vietnamese supporters, and they were hesitant to join an antiwar movement whose success would bring with it a communist victory. They looked for a third way, a noncommunist left capable of ruling in Saigon—a political option that should have existed but didn't. I belonged to the second generation of *Dissent*-niks; I didn't know the names of the murdered leftists, and I came early on to believe that the cruelties of the American war were probably worse than the cruelties to come if the war failed.

So there was division among the editors and writers of *Dissent*. I took this to be an honorable division among liberal socialists (and liberal democrats) facing a very hard choice between an ugly war and a cruel politics. Although I argued that opposition to the American war had to come first, my connection to those leftists who opposed the war because they hoped for a communist victory, and who carried Vietcong flags at all our demonstrations, was torturous and temporary. They were illiberal leftists, too certain of their politics, insufficiently worried about endings. For the long run, I preferred the company of the older *Dissent*-niks who remembered the names of their murdered comrades.

That was my politics; I inherited it without having lived through the ideological battles between Stalinists and Trotskyists or ever having chafed at the narrowness of sectarianism. But opposition to the illiberal left still left a lot of room for a leftist pluralism.

Years later, when the founders were gone and Mitchell Cohen and I were co-editors, the *Dissent*-niks were once again divided by a war—the impending invasion of Iraq in 2003. Some of us defended the war in the name of left internationalism. The overthrow of a brutal authoritarian regime justified the use of force even by a country with a right-wing government and even given the uncertainty about what would follow military success. This was indeed an old left position. Just as the Red Army marched on Warsaw to bring communism to Poland, now the American army was marching on Baghdad to bring democracy to Iraq. Some of the neoconservatives who supported the war were ex-Trotskyists who were, perhaps, acting from memory. The *Dissent*-niks who joined them, briefly and uneasily, followed the lead of Kanan Makiya, an Iraqi exile who had written for the magazine, who argued that the war was worthwhile so long as there was a 10 percent chance of creating a democratic Iraq.

Most of us, and this was my own position, invoked the classic liberal doctrine of nonintervention first enunciated by John Stuart Mill: the overthrow of an authoritarian regime has to be the work of its subjects. Liberals and leftists might help with political and moral support, and individuals might join the struggle as volunteers, but foreign armies should stay out, since they were unlikely to be able to establish and sustain a democratic government.

In the months before the invasion, we carried articles supporting and opposing the war, for which we were harshly criticized by people I think of as illiberal socialists. They thought this was the right time to purge supporters of the war from the magazine and to expel them from the editorial board or, at least, encourage them to resign. We didn't do that. I thought the demand a rancorous response to comrades who disagreed. Instead, we hung together despite the disagreements and continued to argue with one another after the war and throughout the ensuing occupation.

Many of the war's opponents claimed that the mayhem and sectarian bloodshed that followed the invasion proved they were right—which is probably right. But they went on to call for immediate American disengagement from Iraq and everywhere else—which isn't right. In a remarkable novel (*The Rope,* 2016) about the postwar period, Kanan Makiya argued (it was that kind of a novel) that the American invasion, by overthrowing Saddam Hussein, gave the Iraqi people an opportunity to create a decent regime. Instead, the Shi'a leaders preferred revenge and domination, hence the mayhem and the sectarian wars. That account reduced, but only partially, American responsibility for what was always a possible, even a likely, outcome of the invasion. And then the United States found itself unable to prevent, and soon engaged in, the wars of Sunni and Shi'a Iraqis, with no prospect of anything that could be called a victory.

But getting out of Iraq had its own complexities, moral as well as military. At *Dissent,* we produced a book called *Getting Out* (2009), with chapters about the British disengagement from its American colonies and from India, the French withdrawal from Algeria, the American withdrawal from the Philippines, and the Israeli withdrawal from Gaza, all to help us think about an American disengagement from Iraq. In the book we argued that there were responsibilities that followed from colonization and imperialism, and from wars, just and unjust. In Iraq, we had a responsibility to protect the people who worked with the occupation, our collaborators, and also the men and women who came out as democrats, trade unionists, and feminists under American cover. By "we" above, I mean Americans, but we American socialists surely had a special obligation to defend Iraqi comrades who were themselves defending human rights at great risk. Some feminists among them opposed the 2011 withdrawal of American forces, which they took, given the strength of the Sunni and Shi'a militias, as a near death sentence. What should we (the smaller "we") have done then? Liberal socialists acknowledged the difficulty. A single-minded demand for American disengagement everywhere can't be the right answer.

The demand that leftists who supported the Iraq invasion be excluded from the left is only one example, a minor one, of a kind of moral panic that occasionally afflicts the left. Every once in a while, we live through a period when those accused of ideological heresy or political faithlessness or simply of not being radical enough are driven out of the current version of the "woke" left. Or they are required to confess their misdeeds and abjectly repudiate their mistaken views. Sometimes they bravely refuse to do either. As the secular equivalent of sinners, they are treated roughly the way seventeenth-century Puritans treated people who fornicated or went to the theater.

The "struggle sessions" of China's Cultural Revolution, where class enemies were ritually denounced by their fellow citizens, provide an extreme example of this leftist affliction. The citizens reciting the required denunciations knew that if they didn't join the "struggle," they might find themselves among its targets, hence the fierceness of their participation. American examples, happily, are less fierce; the stakes are much lower. But I remember one incident worth recounting. In the early days of the revival of the Democratic Socialists of America (DSA), in 2016 and immediately after, when the organization was joined by many new (and very young) socialists eager to prove their commitment, it was revealed that a member of the recently elected National Political Committee (NPC) had been involved, long ago, in an effort to organize a police union. This man (I will call him DF) was an old militant, a mainstay of DSA during the famine years, who had worked for Bernie Sanders's presidential campaign. He was, in other words, a comrade. The Communication Workers of America, a more left union, had asked him to try to organize the police, and he had done that with some success. The response to this revelation (he insisted that his union work was well known before the election) was an onslaught of demands that he be expelled from the NPC. The police were enemies of the people, and DF was effectively one of them. A few years later, I googled his name and found resolutions from many DSA chapters denouncing him in pretty much the same language, as if the members felt that DSA was somehow morally contaminated by his very presence and that they would be contaminated too if they didn't hurry to join the campaign against him. He was expelled from the NPC and pretty much isolated within DSA. Only the old-timers defended him, perhaps remembering a past they regretted.

The adjective "liberal" means that there has to be room for socialists to disagree among themselves—to disagree about what Ignazio Silone called "the choice of comrades," about the strategy and tactics of the struggle, and about which compromises are necessary and which are "rotten." There will then be many versions of a socialist politics, and we should expect to find parties, unions, and magazines of different sorts competing for members (subscribers, too) and influence within a liberal democratic framework. The competition will be continuous because, finally, "liberal" means that "socialism is not a static and abstract ideal that can one day be completely realized" (Rosselli again), not by struggle at home and certainly not by force abroad. The world around us changes; new inequalities emerge in place of old ones; we never stop arguing among ourselves; the messiah doesn't come; the revolution is postponed. Or we live through a revolution that we can't control and end up with a new fight against dictatorship and terror. Socialism is steady work.

As Eduard Bernstein suggested long ago, the movement is more important than the end. Or, as Rosselli wrote, "The end lives in our present actions." It had better live there, since there isn't any other place. The adjective "liberal" is hostile to actual endings.

Many socialists overpromised what those endings would bring. They told ethnic, religious, and racial minorities what they more famously told women—that the success of the socialist revolution would mean the end of all oppression. The triumph of the working class would be, at the same time, a universal liberation. "Class rule would forever be at an end," wrote August Bebel, the leader of German social democracy, "and with it the rule of man over woman." It followed, then, that any political struggle against social and economic discrimination or political subjugation—by women or Jews or Blacks or Poles or Slovaks—would detract from the general and all-important struggle of the working class. Revolutionary energy should be narrowly focused, not dissipated in parochial political activity addressing what were marginal forms of oppression.

But Bebel doesn't seem to have accepted this latter dictum. When he wrote in his book *Women and Socialism* (1879) that the status of women determined the level of civilization, he provided a critical principle that would presumably show different civilizational levels in different times and places. (The book was published in the United States with the title *Women under Socialism* and was translated by Daniel DeLeon, who denounced Bebel's critique of monogamy, which in its pure form, DeLeon thought, represents the highest level of civilization.) Given the centrality of women's status, feminist political work must be worthwhile whatever the state of the class struggle. Perhaps Bebel believed that; at any rate, he had supported the creation of the General German Woman's Association in 1865—an organization that was not subject to socialist or working-class discipline.

I don't think that Bebel was a liberal socialist. He didn't adopt Bernstein's revisionism, and he certainly wasn't hostile to (or skeptical about) endings. But insofar as he supported an independent feminism, he suggested what the politics of liberal socialists should look like. Bebel is also credited—probably wrongly, but that doesn't matter here—with the claim that "anti-Semitism is the socialism of fools." That line would seem to require a struggle here and now against anti-Semitism. Without that, the triumph of socialism might turn out to be the triumph of fools.

Contemporary socialists watched the reemergence of this old perversion of socialist doctrine during the (thankfully) brief reign of Jeremy Corbyn as head of the British Labor Party. Under the cover that Corbyn provided, large numbers of his followers, the party's hard left, readily turned their hatred of Israel and their "third worldist" politics into an explicit anti-Semitism. The extent of the turning was carefully documented in an unofficial 2019 Report to the Labor Party by Alan Johnson, a loyal member of the party, and his argument was later strongly affirmed by an official government-sponsored study. What was most disturbing about the Corbyn years was the extreme reluctance of many leftists, who would have said that they abhorred anti-Semitism, to condemn the anti-Semites. They seem to have thought that Corbyn's leftist program was too important to be criticized for something as minor as Jew hatred. I am sure they also believed that the success of the program would bring an end to this and every other sort of hatred. They were not sufficiently skeptical about endings.

Socialists are defined, according to Rosselli, by their "active attachment . . . to the cause of the poor and the oppressed." This attachment cannot itself be defined by a comprehensive doctrine; it is not expressed in a single, correct ideological position that can be adopted and enforced by a vanguard of knowers. "Grief will result," Rosselli says, "from trying to fetter a movement with a development spanning centuries, a movement irrepressibly polyphonic, to a given philosophical creed." Certainly, we have had a lot of grief over the years from trying to do that. Liberal socialists will be skeptical even about the creeds to which they are committed; a touch of irony is inherent in all liberal commitments.

The central creedal commitment is to equality: the overcoming of poverty by the poor themselves, by working men and women organized in the labor movement and in socialist parties. The goal is the end of oppression, the creation of a society from which the steep hierarchies that we know today and every kind of deference and humiliation have been banished. Writing in the 1990s, the Italian socialist Norberto Bobbio (who stands in a direct line from Carlo Rosselli) argued that equality was "the highest . . . ideal of an ordered, just, and happy community." But in accordance with his own liberal socialism, Bobbio insisted that he wasn't an "egalitarianist" who believed that everyone should be equal in everything (*Left and Right*, 1996). Equality was a relative, not an absolute, ideal. We have to argue about what it means. How much equality? Achieved by what methods? With reference to what social goods?

Although liberal socialists are not "egalitarianist," they are serious about equality—more so, generally, than liberal democrats. Socialists and social democrats, even when they are no longer Marxists, are more ready to recognize the ways in which specific forms of inequality are embedded in long-standing practices and institutions. Racial inequality especially is "structural," which means that it doesn't exist only at the level of individual or collective prejudice and that it can't be ended by color blindness and race neutrality. Affirmative action, a good social democratic policy, is helpful, but it has to be accompanied by long-term transformations in education, housing, and employment. By itself, affirmative action doesn't change the hierarchical character of capitalist society; it just moves some people into higher positions. It makes for a more defensible hierarchy, but not yet a just society.

What would a just society look like—egalitarian but not egalitarianist? The underlying issue might best be stated differently: How much inequality is compatible with the vision of a just society? Human beings are different from one another, and if we refuse to repress the differences, if we reject the Procrustean bed, they will produce further differences in achievements and relative standing in every area of social life. That will be true even when the differences are no longer class or racially driven. Let's consider now how those differences might play out in our critique of capitalism. I will begin with a story, first told in the mainstream press and then retold with relish across the left.

Thinking ahead, imagining possible pandemics, the Obama administration signed a contract with a small (think startup or upstart) company making cheap, portable ventilators. A much bigger company that produced big, heavy, and expensive ventilators, fearing competition, then bought the small company, shut down the production

of the cheap, portable ventilators, and canceled the government contract, claiming that it wasn't profitable enough. Government regulators approved the merger of the two companies, apparently without
questioning its likely consequence.

Here is a story of predatory capitalism, profit-driven economic
behavior, and a laissez-faire state—so it was told, and so it is. But no
one retelling the story seems to have noticed that it is also about the
value of the entrepreneurial enterprise represented by the small company and its portable ventilators. In this case, the entrepreneurs sold
out, took the money, and ran—standard economic behavior in a capitalist society. They didn't insist on continuing to produce their ventilators for the sake of the common good. But it was the government
regulators who should have made sure that the merged company delivered the ventilators that the Obama people had contracted for.
They are the ones who failed to serve the common good. Still, even if
they had been committed social democrats, they couldn't have produced the ventilators themselves.

Entrepreneurs are necessary; they aren't necessarily benevolent;
they produce and sell a lot of junk—but also things like those portable ventilators. We need to make sure there is space for them to do
what they do, space for individual innovation and risk-taking. There
has to be motivation, too, not just money but also honor and celeb-
rity. It is no affront to liberal socialist egalitarianism, as I understand
it, if the entrepreneur who sells portable ventilators makes more
money than I do and is more widely known than I am. The socialist
state should not interfere with "small-scale ownership," as George
Orwell wrote in *The Lion and the Unicorn* (1941).

Income differentiation (within decent limits, fixed by tax policy) is
defensible so long as the other person's money isn't convertible into
power over you and me. Convertibility is the key: What can money

buy and what can't it buy? Today, in the United States, it can buy almost anything, but that isn't a necessary feature even of our own almighty dollar; there are purchases that ought to be barred and others that are harmless. If successful entrepreneurs can afford a more expensive vacation than I can; if they can collect first editions of rare books and I can't; if they buy the newest fashions and I am hopelessly unfashionable—all that is compatible with a just society. But if they can buy medical care that isn't available to me; if they get legal representation in civil and criminal cases that I don't get; if they have influence with government agencies that I don't have—that is unjust. The latter examples reveal the economic inequality that matters, which is the inequality we currently live with.

Having more money than I have isn't a crime; nor is it a crime to go shopping with that money—so long as certain sales are barred. You shouldn't be able to go shopping for a human being, or for a judge or a senator, or (I wish) for a gun, or for machines whose safety hasn't been checked by experts, or for inflammable pajamas or contaminated foods. The market has to be regulated. But I have never understood the left critique of consumerism, as if there is something wrong with shopping itself or with the desire for beautiful things. Shopping is a common human activity, widely attested in ancient Greece and Babylonia. The Middle Eastern shuk (souk) is a shopper's paradise; Western tourists, many of whom disdain the name "consumer," enjoy its wonders.

When the union came to America's industrial towns, and workers suddenly had more money than they had ever had before, they became consumers. The first thing they bought, merchants in my hometown reported, was a washing machine (for the wife, of course), but they also went shopping more widely. My father managed a jewelry store, and he told me stories of steelworker families coming in to buy a necklace or bracelet for a sixteen-year-old daughter—they were proud shoppers. That is an achievement of the organized left, which too many leftists don't value.

We should think of political power in the same way we think of the uses of money. Democratic elections are a way of distributing power unequally. Not only are there winners and losers; most of us aren't even candidates. But, again, that isn't unjust; it's no threat to general equality so long as power is limited—that is, not convertible into privileges denied to ordinary citizens. Just as there are blocked uses of economic power, so there have to be blocked uses of political power. The two go together. Wealthy men and women can't buy victory in civil suits; judges can't take their bribes and deliver corrupt verdicts. Elected officials can't appoint their unqualified relatives to administrative positions or invest in companies they are supposed to regulate.

The former Soviet Union was a place where political power was radically unblocked; members of the Communist Party enjoyed all sorts of benefits that ordinary citizens couldn't imagine. The United States today is a place where there are too few blocked uses of economic power. The largely failed efforts to regulate campaign finance suggest the power of money to prevent its own blockage and then to influence the outcomes of our elections. More generally, Americans have failed to constrain the role of money as it was described, long ago, by William Shakespeare. It is the universal pander. It puts everything up for sale.

The case is the same with what we now call "meritocracy." There is nothing wrong, from the standpoint of equality, with awarding positions in the civil service or in a university or a hospital to talented or competent men and women—assuming a search procedure uncorrupted by money or power, or race or gender. And then these people can campaign, say, for political office, claiming that their talents will make for better government. Let the voters decide whether the claim has merit. But we shouldn't consider anything like John Stuart Mill's proposal that we give a double vote to men and women with university degrees on the grounds that what they have learned makes them politically wiser. It doesn't. I know some highly educated and very learned people who are political idiots. Learned men and women should be respected in their fields, where their learning is relevant, not beyond that, where it isn't.

The civil service exam was invented to make sure that qualification and not wealth, family influence, party loyalty, or whiteness (or maleness) wins someone a position of public trust. The exams must be closely focused on the work that the candidate will have to do if appointed. We don't follow the ancient Chinese practice and appoint someone to a job in the Social Security Administration, say, because he tests well in the knowledge of classical texts. It is not intellectual cultivation but technical competence that counts. And once someone is in office, with his or her merits recognized, we must beware of what Shakespeare called the "insolence of office." Official positions should never open paths to forms of authority and privilege that have nothing to do with the work of the office.

The work of the office is often important, however, and when it is well done, it should be rewarded, if not with wealth and power, then with respect and praise. I singled out teachers in the chapter on liberal democrats as men and women holding important offices in our society who are insufficiently respected—perhaps because they spend their lives working with children, most of whom will never qualify for any high meritocratic position. But that is why teachers are so important: they are the agents of democratic equality, recognizing the worth of all their students and teaching them to recognize each other's worth. They work to produce citizens and also to encourage the effort and honor the achievements of all their students. They look for merit in all its forms. Themselves qualified professionals, they are also, if they are doing their job, and whether they know it or not, liberal socialists.

So, under liberal socialism, people with money can choose among the full range of available commodities; they can buy and enjoy whatever can rightly be bought—and nothing else. People with power can take pleasure in making decisions about the common good, but not about their own and their relatives' good—and always with the knowledge that they are democratically accountable. And people with talent can enjoy the exercise of their talents in all the fields to which those talents apply. Nothing more.

In the 1980s and 1990s, *Dissent* carried a number of articles defending market socialism. The defense was mostly couched in pragmatic terms: this was, as the Scots economist Alec Nove wrote in 1985, "feasible socialism." It was politically feasible (and, I would add, morally desirable) because it recognized the value of the market in regulating supply and demand and so avoided the totalizing tendencies of centralized state planning. It was a liberal socialism, setting limits on political power; it also described a pluralist economy where economic power would be similarly limited.

Market socialists imagined a mix of corporate, company, and business formations. There would be socialized industries, organized at different levels (national, municipal) and managed in different ways. Some would have boards with representative workers and consumers as well as investors; some would have government-appointed boards dealing with strong unions.

There would also be worker-owned companies, whose collective self-determination would produce different market outcomes. Some would be efficiently run, some not; some would choose quality of life over productivity; some would invest their profits in new technology, others in day care or a nursery school for the children of the workers. The worker-owners would end up with different incomes, just like private owners today, but there is considerable evidence that they would also possess a much greater sense of self-worth than would employees who have no part in collective decision-making. And, of course, everyone would be protected by a strong welfare state.

Finally, there would be privately owned businesses—the products of entrepreneurial activity (remember the cheap ventilators)— which would succeed and fail as in capitalist (and precapitalist) economies. Given a socialist safety net, failure would be less dangerous than it is today, but there would still be risks involved. Individual entrepreneurs would be on their own, free to seek out danger or avoid it. Risk is "bracing," the English socialist R. H. Tawney writes, "if it is voluntarily undertaken because in that case a man balances probable gains and losses and stakes his brains and character on success." By contrast, in a capitalist society workers gain little or nothing if the enterprise succeeds but are sure to bear the "sufferings of failure" if it doesn't— while the "gains" of a successful enterprise don't only increase the owner's wealth but can be converted into political power and social privilege. The success of entrepreneurial activity in a liberal socialist society would be of lesser consequence but still worth the risks involved. It would be a sad socialism that discouraged economic (and other) adventures.

Liberal socialism has nothing to do with five-year plans, coerced uniformity, or a closing down of the space for individual initiative. The aim instead is a pluralized economy and a more cooperative society so that citizens can recognize each other and engage with each other as equals. As I wrote in 1983, in *Spheres of Justice,* "This is the lively hope named by the word *equality:* no more bowing and scraping, fawning and toadying, no more fearful trembling, no more high-and-mightiness, no more masters, no more slaves." And since there will always be men and women aspiring to be high and mighty, the only way to get to a liberal socialist society is to keep on getting there.

The catastrophic potential of climate change should lead us to worry about just keeping on. Warming temperatures, rising waters, ever-fiercer storms, burning forests, farmland turning into desert—we face unprecedented dangers. These are the result of our own activity, much of it designed by good people and aimed at making our lives better, easier, more comfortable. Now hardship looms: everyone (almost everyone) knows that urgent action is necessary, and everyone is afraid of acting urgently. Not only vested interests are at risk but also the jobs and homes of ordinary citizens, along with all our modern conveniences.

Many people claim that we need a global government to deal with the crisis. But no global government is in sight. The necessary decisions will have to be made, or not made, in the existing world of sovereign states. It is in those sovereign states that the critical battles about climate change are right now being fought. I can't say that they are being won anywhere. So far, the record shows that the best responses, still woefully inadequate, have come from states with liberal democratic or social democratic governments (or from states with a tradition of state regulation produced by social democratic governments in the past). A strong and democratically accountable state seems the most likely agent for environmental engagement. Private enterprise, corporate decision-making, won't work; the incentives aren't right. Indeed, there are no incentives at all for corporations engaged in activities that produce carbon emissions on a large scale unless a social democratic government intervenes with regulations, tax policies, fines, and subsidies. But the state alone, unaccountable, won't deal with the crisis either, as we know from the experience of authoritarian socialist governments in Eastern Europe and the Soviet

Union. Nor will a weak state, subject to capitalist capture, do what is necessary; the recent history of the United States is evidence enough.

In a pinch, faced with present, not just forecast, dangers, we might well turn to an authoritarian ruler who could act against the vested interests, override all opposition, including democratic opposition, and save us or, more likely, some of us, from the destructiveness of an avenging nature. But if we want to be saved before that, we should be looking for a democratic state with strong regulatory powers, accustomed to using them but publicly accountable for how they are used. There will be hardships involved in the transition to an economy fueled by sun and wind rather than by coal and oil, and the hardest hardships will fall on workers employed in the industries now producing or dependent on coal and oil. Only a government trusted by the people, visibly committed to their welfare and responsive to their complaints, can manage the transition without brutal coercion. We will need massive investment in alternative fuels and in infrastructure generally to provide jobs and a sense of security to people displaced elsewhere, as well as retraining programs that are geared to the newly available jobs, and a welfare system capable of dealing with all the likely transitional troubles.

To combine entrepreneurial innovation and state planning, economic change and working-class well-being, sacrifice and social equality, climate control and individual liberty—none of this is easy. Success won't be steady, nor will fairness be sustained at every point. But democracy and socialism in their liberal—constrained and pluralist—versions seem to hold out the best hope for meeting the danger.

There is a further argument: liberal democrats and socialists are, as recent political engagements demonstrate, far more likely than their illiberal opponents to believe in the "steady work" of modern science. And, maybe, the need to deal democratically and rationally with climate change will push us ahead on the long march to social justice. Steady work, also.

4

Liberal Nationalists
and Internationalists

Nationalists are people who put the interests of their own nation first. Liberal nationalists are people who do that and recognize the right of other people to do the same thing—and who then insist that all the "firsts" accommodate one another. They acknowledge the legitimacy and the legitimate interests of the different nations. Liberal nationalism is probably the oldest form of nationalism, dating from the heady days of Guiseppe Mazzini's Young Italy, founded in 1831 with the aim of creating a unified and independent Italian republic. Mazzini proved his right to the adjective "liberal" by helping to found Young Poland, Young Germany, and Young Switzerland, all of them committed to national liberation and self-determination. The recognition of a plurality of collective "selves" is the key idea of liberal nationalism.

Mazzini also created Young Europe, a project with a more distant end in view. He imagined a future Europe as a concert of nations and invoked the image of an orchestra where each nation "played" its own culture; the result, he thought, would be a beautiful symphony. Marx used the same imagery to describe the harmonious cooperation of workers in a communist factory, and Horace Kallen, the American social theorist, thought that cultural pluralism would be, as a friendly critic wrote, "the orchestration of difference." It is a great idea but not a plausible metaphor.

Years ago, a smart student in one of my political theory courses wrote a paper on what you might call the government of orchestras and identified the tyranny of the conductor as the most common regime. Without an authoritarian conductor, he argued, harmony would most often give way to cacophony. So it has been with the concert of Europe for most of the years since Mazzini wrote. Liberal nationalism turns out to be a more difficult project than it seemed when Italians, Poles, Germans, and Swiss were Young. It requires a political struggle against illiberal nationalists at home and complicated diplomatic dealings with self-regarding nation-states abroad.

As liberal democrats set limits on the power of triumphalist majorities, and as liberal socialists set limits on the authority of theory-obsessed vanguards, liberal nationalists set limits on the collective narcissism of nations. The goal is peaceful coexistence.

We defenders of the adjective "liberal" don't deny that majorities have rights, or that theoretical knowledge is important, or that national belonging is a genuine value. But we defend minorities against majority tyranny and ordinary activists against vanguard arrogance. And we defend nations that need states against any opposing nation-states—Kurds, Palestinians, and Tibetans against Turkey, Israel, and China, for example—but we do this without denying the national rights of ethnic Turks, Israeli Jews, and Han Chinese.

By contrast, people calling themselves cosmopolitans condemn all nationalisms; they deny the value of national membership and surrender the hope of a concert of nations. Cosmopolitanism is more a philosophical doctrine than a political ideology, but it does nonetheless press toward a certain kind of politics. It is obviously hostile to nationalism, but it is also hostile to democracy. Its defenders do not acknowledge the value of the enclosed political spaces—like city-states and nation-states—that are the natural home of democratic politics, indeed, its only home. It is hard to imagine how cosmopolitans might organize a political party or hold an election among citizens of the world.

Can there be a liberal cosmopolitanism? Since cosmopolitan philosophers recognize only rights-bearing individuals, surely they should be called liberals. But most of these individuals set a high value on their particular memberships and identify themselves as French, Japanese, Arab, Norwegian, and so on, and not as citizens of the world. The refusal to value these identifications and the pluralism that results from them seems to me illiberal. It prefers men and women as they should be to men and women as they are—who would have to be forced to be cosmopolitan. The billions of people who inhabit the world aren't by history, biography, or habit, and probably not by nature, world citizens. A global state could rule over them only if it were brutally repressive of (almost) everyone's national identity and ethnic loyalty. Remember Immanuel Kant's description of such a state: it would be a "soulless despotism." To avoid that despotism, liberal cosmopolitans would have to make their peace with liberal nationalists.

The name of the peace is internationalism, a term that describes or, better, mandates, not the abolition of borders, but cooperation and solidarity across borders. Achieving internationalism isn't as easy as socialists once thought when they believed that "workers have no country" and that nationally based socialist parties would support one another against their own governments. In the lead-up to World War I, workers across Europe chose their nation (and its government) over their class, even if that meant fighting against fellow workers. Perhaps class solidarity across impending and then actual battle lines was too severe a test of internationalism. Opposition to the war might better have focused on universal rather than class-based ideas of justice. The war was a struggle for colonies in Africa and hegemony in Europe, unjust on all sides. It was the farther left, bourgeois intellectuals and militants, who opposed the war for those reasons; they had little support among the workers until, in Germany, the war seemed lost.

Democratic socialists do better when they recognize the national loyalties of their people and build strong national parties. Truth to tell, they have not been successful anywhere except in the nation-state. The home of democracy turns out to be, naturally enough, the home of social democracy. There socialists have found the only political space within which they have been able to win significant political victories. David Miller has made this point repeatedly and well: "The welfare state—and indeed, programs to protect minority rights—have always been *national* projects, justified on the basis that members of a community must protect one another and guarantee one another equal respect." Miller goes on to argue (in his book *On Nationality,* 1995) that when national identities weaken, corporate elites have a free hand to enact their own agenda. The glory years of social democracy were also years when the European nation-state was strong and when its politics reflected a sense of shared citizenship and mutuality. By contrast, the United States, the great un-nation, is one of the shoddiest welfare states in the Western world.

From the space of the nation-state, socialists can provide political support for comrades in other countries. Assuming that their commitment to the nation is a liberal commitment, they will also provide support for national liberation movements and for embattled and vulnerable peoples abroad. You might call that liberal internationalism.

What about military support? I have already argued against sending armies across borders for the sake of regime change—as in the case of Iraq in 2003. Individual volunteers are something else. The Communist International was able to send volunteer fighters to Spain in the 1930s, recruited from German, French, Polish, and other national parties. The American participants proudly called themselves the

Lincoln Brigade. Nothing like that is possible on the left today. Instead, Islamist volunteers from many countries are fighting in places like Iraq and Syria. But they aren't internationalists; they don't recognize national borders. They are religious cosmopolitans, believers in a borderless caliphate.

Since the mid-1970s, I have defended the idea and sometimes the practice of humanitarian intervention as an internationalist project. I am not talking about a socialist internationalism. The use of armed force to stop a massacre is best understood as a defense of life and liberty, hence a liberal undertaking. Still, one of the few recent examples, the war in Kosovo, was the work of a Labor government in Great Britain, the Socialists in France, a coalition of Social Democrats and Greens in Germany, and the Democratic Party of the Left in Italy, and—militarily necessary but the weakest link politically—President Bill Clinton's "third way" in the United States. It was the work of a multinational left. Nonetheless, humanitarian intervention is a liberal politics: its goal is not an egalitarian replacement of a murderous regime but only a non-murderous replacement. It aims to open up possibilities. After doing that, liberal democrats and liberal socialists abroad will look for allies inside the country and support them in any (nonmilitary) way they can—and this support will be, again, an example of liberal internationalism.

Some people on the left oppose humanitarian intervention—at least when it is or might be undertaken by the United States or by former colonial powers like Great Britain or France. It is helpful, then, to consider the Vietnamese in Cambodia, the Indians in East Pakistan, now Bangladesh, and the Tanzanians in Uganda. The rulers of these intervening states were, all of them, nationalists, and they probably had their own nation's security in mind when they sent their troops into a neighboring country. But they were also internationalists, defending the lives of foreigners. We could say that they recognized the value of the borders they crossed by crossing them only in the emergency of mass murder.

The adjective "liberal" turns nationalism into a universalist doctrine. Yael Tamir makes the point very clearly in her book *Liberal Nationalism* (1995): "The acknowledgment of the importance of cultural membership and . . . the assertion of a general right to cultural and national self-determination must be at the center of any [liberal] theory of nationalism." One meaning of this "general right" is that all nations must recognize the claims of the others and make room for the nation that comes next.

The English political theorist Thomas Hobbes, thinking of the plight of refugees fleeing famine or persecution, writes that people living in neighboring states may have to "inhabit more closely together" to make room for the refugees. You could call that the moral requirement of a (very) liberal nationalism, but it is a hard demand to make; taking in refugees has never required such a clustering of the natives. There is another demand of liberal nationalism that is easier to make: imperial nation-states that have expanded at the expense of other nations must withdraw from those others and contract their size. I doubt that there is such a thing as liberal imperialism, although there certainly are more and less brutal versions of imperial rule. If there were such a thing, it would be an imperialism genuinely committed to its future contraction, to making room for the subject nations.

The radical defenders of Little England in the late nineteenth and early twentieth centuries were anti-imperialists and, at the same time, good liberal nationalists. The call for Greater Israel today, extending from the river to the sea, is an example of illiberal nationalism, while the defenders of "little Israel" are liberal Zionists—as is Tamir, who invokes the memory of the Girondins in the French Revolution. They wanted to create free nation-states, she writes, "in the territories that France had conquered."

Liberal nationalists are defenders of national liberation even or especially when the liberation movement is opposed by their own nation's nationalists. When French leftists supported Algerian independence, they were also supporting a fervently nationalist and illiberal Algerian political movement, the National Liberation Front (FLN). Since they believed that Algerian independence required the end of the French empire, but not of the French state, they were, consciously or not, acting like liberal nationalists—sustaining their own national project while accommodating the nation that comes next. If these leftists had been liberal democrats or liberal socialists, however, they would have condemned FLN terrorism exactly as they condemned the terrorism of the French colonial army and police.

Terrorism—the deliberate killing of innocent people for a political purpose—is to national liberation what dictatorship and repression are to revolutionary socialism: the chosen path of illiberal militants. I have lived with arguments about terrorism all my political life, since these arguments were central to Zionist politics in the 1930s and 1940s. I was too young to join the arguments in those years, but I inherited them later on, and I have written extensively about them from the inside, so to speak. It is worth noting that the Jewish advocates and practitioners of terrorism in Mandatory Palestine were right-wing, even far-right Zionists. Their strongest opponents were Zionists of the left. Years later, it was leftists, or people calling themselves leftists, who were the chief terrorists, as in Algeria and Palestine. The chief apologists for terrorism were also men and women of the European and American left.

Against them, I have often quoted a lovely line from Trotsky: "Terrorists want to make the people happy without the participation of the people." Terrorism is an elitist politics—the work of the heroic few—and therefore an authoritarian politics. It represents a turning away from the kinds of struggle that we might call "democracy-seeking": mass mobilization, general strikes, nonviolent protest. Terrorists commonly claim that their decision to target innocent people is a "last resort." We can see the falsehood of this claim if we imagine a meeting where liberation militants are deciding what to do. A group of men (it is almost always men) sit around a table arguing: some support a terrorist strategy but others oppose it. The few accounts we have were written by the opponents, whom I will call liberal nationalists. The would-be terrorists insist that there is nothing else to do; the opponents have a list of alternatives. In fact, there always are other things to do; terrorism has more often been a first than a last resort.

Liberal nationalists are bound to respect the life and liberty of innocent people. The bomb in the café or on the bus would be anathema to them. The ban on terror, like the ban on torture, is as close to absolute as liberals can get. That does not imply a weaker commitment to national liberation, but rather a commitment to achieve liberation only with the participation of the people. Terrorism will produce, as the Algerian case suggests, an authoritarian regime—the heroic few ruling over the disorganized many. A liberal liberation would open the way for democracy.

Many leftists who defend national liberation in places like Algeria or Vietnam do not think of themselves as nationalists. They have a principled opposition, not always apparent in their everyday politics, to the nation-state. Insofar as the state belongs to or reflects the culture of the majority, they argue, it cannot be a liberal democracy. All the minorities will necessarily be oppressed—and there are no nation-states without minority populations. Indeed, even if there were entirely homogeneous states, they couldn't rightly remain so, given the legitimate demands of migrants and refugees to come in. Do the French, then, or the Norwegians or the Japanese have any moral claim to a state of their own?

Consider the Norwegian case (as I have often done in arguments about nationalism). In 1905, Norway seceded from its ninety-one-year-old union with Sweden. This was a nationalist secession. The Norwegians were afraid that they were losing their language, history, and culture. The state they established is, among other things, a little engine for the production and reproduction of Norwegianness. I do not know of any significant protests against the existence of this nation-state. Of course, the Norwegians have to treat the aboriginal people of the North, the Samis, fairly, as equal citizens, and they have to take in their share of asylum seekers and refugees. But even if they do all that, Norway will still be Norwegian. It won't be anything like America, a "democracy of nationalities," as Kallen called it, where the state is an engine whose only purpose is (or should be) to produce citizens committed to constitutional democracy—and not to promote the culture of any national or ethnic group. It is a curious fact that many left-wing critics of the nation-state seem to think that the model country is America, even if they are also fierce opponents of every aspect of American society and every feature of American foreign policy.

Much of the recent discussion about, and much of the critique of, the nation-state has focused on a single case: the State of Israel. Everything I know and every opinion I have about nationalism comes from my engagement with Israel and my visits there. Well, not everything: as a graduate student I took a course on nationalism and wrote a long paper on the connections between Indian nationalism and Indian communism. My first academic engagement with liberation movements and with national majorities and minorities was not with

Israel, then, but with India. My sympathies in the late 1950s were with Nehruvian liberal nationalism: one Indian state for Hindus and Muslims.

Nehru did not imagine India as a bi-national state. He thought of Hindus and Muslims as members of religious, not national, communities, and like most liberals and leftists of his time, he was sure that religious belief was fading away in the face of what he called "reason and science." Hindu nationalists, the right-wing advocates of Hindutva, were among his chief opponents. In the 1920s and 1930s, they identified with European Zionists, who had also, they thought, fused religion and nationality. At the time, this identification wasn't plausible, since Zionism was a radically secular and increasingly socialist ideology. But it was an ominous sign for days to come.

One aspiration common to Zionism and Nehru's Indian nationalism and to every other national liberation movement is to create "new" men and women who, as Gandhi wrote, are able to manage their own affairs, free of traditionalist passivity and deference, and fit for self-determination and a proud citizenship. The Zionist case is especially revealing given the militants' view of the old Jew: stooped, fearful, physically weak, humbly deferential. Zionist iconography in the pre-state and early state years had a standard form. I remember the posters from my own teen years: a young man, a young woman, side by side, their faces handsome, their bodies sturdy, muscular, a little square; he is holding a shovel, she a hoe; they are looking over beautifully planted fields into the future. After centuries of landlessness, the new Jew was a pioneer and a farmer, as in the comically rhymed couplet from that time: "Who says that Jews cannot be farmers? / Spit on those who would so harm us." These farmers were ready to fight as well as to work in the fields: straight, strong, unafraid.

I found the images inspiring. I guess I wasn't yet a liberal Zionist, skeptical, wondering where among these new Jews we would find intellectuals to sit in the cafes of Tel Aviv and argue about the shape of the Jewish future, or musicians for the Israel Philharmonic Orchestra. I eventually came, without giving up the need for newness, to appreciate (some of) the old Jews.

Perhaps the most striking feature of the new Jews was their language. They spoke Hebrew, a language used only for prayer and study, now resurrected as a language of the street. The resurrection was the work of one man, Eliezer Ben-Yehudah, who insisted that a national revival required a national language, one in which Jews from every part of the Diaspora could talk to one another. Ben-Yehudah's singular role has been questioned by revisionist historians, rightly, I am sure. But his is the story that I grew up with, and I will stick with it here. It is famously reported that when he got off the boat in Jaffa in 1881, he informed his wife that henceforth they would speak only Hebrew. Their son was the first child in the modern world for whom Hebrew was a mother (father) tongue. Ben-Yehudah's vision was rejected by the Orthodox Jews of the Yishuv for whom Hebrew was a sacred language, not to be used in everyday speech. And he was ridiculed by his fellow Zionists, many of whom imagined that the language of the future Jewish state would be German or French. But he was extraordinarily persistent and persuasive. My wife and I, on our first visit to Israel, in 1957, learned about his success on a Tel Aviv street when she, having no Hebrew, tried to ask directions in Yiddish and got a sharp, Ben-Yehudian response: "Dabeir rak Ivrit!" "Speak only Hebrew!"

Ben-Yehudah was not a liberal linguist; he was a language zealot, and I doubt that he could have done what he did had he been any less zealous than he was. At the same time, though, he was a liberal nationalist in the style of Mazzini; he admired the beauty of other national languages and wrote about the "glorious variety and multi-colored splendor" of a world of nations. He only wanted the Jews to be equal participants in the splendor. Still, I don't doubt that his version of radical Hebraism was hard on the Holocaust refugees and the immigrants from Arab countries who arrived in Israel between 1948 and 1955 speaking Yiddish or Ladino (or Polish or Arabic) and who were forcefully told "Dabeir rak Ivrit!"

Zionism was (and is) tested by the nation that came next, not by the Jews who arrived in the years immediately after independence. You might say that the Palestinians are the nation that came first. Already in 1921, after the Arab attacks on Jewish settlements, David Ben-Gurion told his Zionist colleagues: "This is a national movement." Still, it was a movement responding to Zionism, and its nationalism was inchoate—sometimes pan-Arab, less often, I think, narrowly Palestinian. Its leadership was mixed; religious figures and traditional notables, heads of the major families, were the most prominent people in its ranks. National liberation militants, like Yasser Arafat, hadn't yet made an appearance. After the 1948 war, the West Bank was annexed by Jordan, and the Gaza Strip was held by Egypt. There was little room for Palestinian nationalism—the Egyptians tightly controlled it; the Jordanians repressed it. Arafat's Fatah was born far away in the emirate of Kuwait.

Ironically, it was Israel's triumph in 1967 and the occupation of the West Bank and Gaza that cleared the way for an independent Palestinian national liberation movement in the modern secular mode. The model was the Algerian FLN; the favorite theorist of the Fatah militants was Franz Fanon.

This was the situation when I began coming regularly to Israel in the early 1970s. The West Bank and Gaza were occupied territories. Israeli settlement activity in the territories had begun, led by young religious zealots with messianic ideas. Arafat was the acknowledged leader of, and Fatah was the leading political force in, the Palestinian movement. The politics of my Israeli friends, whom I would call liberal nationalists, can be simply described: they opposed the Israeli occupation of the territories. But there were different ideas about how to end the occupation: unilateral withdrawal, the creation of a Palestinian state alongside Israel through talks with the Arab states—or with Arafat and his militants (who at that point were committed to the destruction of Israel)—and the return of the West Bank to Jordan.

The last of these was called the Jordanian solution, and it was much discussed although it had few supporters. After one of my trips to Israel, I visited Washington, DC, for a talk with Zbigniew Brzezinski, President Jimmy Carter's national security advisor, with whom I had taken a course (on the politics of Eastern Europe) in graduate school. He told me that he had once asked Jordan's King Hussein what he thought would be the outcome of an election on the West Bank. The king replied, "If I run the election, I will win the election." Hussein was not a liberal democrat, probably not a democrat of any sort. Still, the Jordanian solution wasn't a bad idea; the unified state that it produced would have had a large Palestinian majority and would surely have morphed over time into a Palestinian state alongside Israel.

Nothing like that was in the cards.

My friends in Israel were old Mapai-niks and Mapam-niks, veterans of two of the original left parties, who looked beyond the euphoria that gripped the country after the 1967 war and opposed all the settlement projects. Some of them might have supported the Jordanian solution, but mostly they came to be advocates of "two states for two peoples." That was a real possibility now that Israel and the Palestinians were face-to-face—although for years neither side had leaders ready to recognize the other. In those years, I visited Israel often and marched and demonstrated with my friends (at their invitation). Then, in 1993, in Oslo and Washington, the fight to end the occupation and create a Palestinian state alongside Israel seemed, briefly, to have been won. I was one of those invited—as a representative of Americans for Peace Now, the support group here in the United States for peaceniks in Israel—to stand on the White House lawn and watch the two sides in the persons of Yitzhak Rabin and Arafat shake hands. That was also a time of euphoria, more sober, I think, than in 1967, not a messianic but a liberal euphoria. We were happy, excited—and worried.

It was a moment to seize, when Rabin should have picked a fight with the settler movement and Arafat should have picked a fight with the advocates of armed resistance. They had to win those fights before a real peace was possible. Both men chose postponement, Rabin for political reasons, Arafat, I suspect, for ideological reasons. And then Rabin was assassinated, the Palestinians launched a terrorist campaign, Bibi Netanyahu won the 1996 election for Israel's prime minister, and the moment was lost.

I won't rehearse the tribulations of the years since. In Israel, two governments, center-left and centrist, neither one long in power, produced proposals for a Palestinian state that didn't meet the expectations of Palestinian nationalists and were rejected—wrongly, I think, if we consider the well-being of ordinary Palestinians (and Israelis). The unilateral Israeli withdrawal from the Gaza Strip brought Hamas to power, split the Palestinian national movement, and led to several inconclusive mini-wars. Long years of right-wing rule in Israel, the daily cruelties of the occupation, and the steady expansion of Jewish settlements on the West Bank aided and abetted by illiberal nationalists have made it harder and harder to imagine a Palestinian state alongside Israel.

Other solutions to the conflict have been proposed, federations and confederations that would, perhaps, meet the basic needs of liberal nationalists on both sides by offering self-determination short of full state sovereignty. But are there enough liberal nationalists on either side to sustain complex arrangements like those? The proposal most favored on the farther left would deny self-determination to both nations and create instead a "state of all its citizens"—not a nation-state of any sort but a kind of America-in-the-Middle-East. The great difficulty with this idea lies in the phrase "all its citizens." Who would these be? Both Jews and Palestinians are committed to the doctrine of "return." The Jews would want the new state to provide, as Israel now does, a refuge for Jews in trouble across the Diaspora. The Palestinians now have their own diaspora; they would want the new state to be open to any diasporic Palestinians who want to come home. The two nations would have to negotiate not only about the constitutional rights and obligations of each one but also, literally, about the population of the country. Two states, each choosing its own immigration policies, might well be easier. Then liberal and illiberal nationalists within each state could compete for power.

Immigration is one of the central issues of nationalist politics. Cosmopolitan philosophers argue for open borders, which would avoid all the long-standing complexities and make it unnecessary to distinguish between fellow nationals and foreigners when shaping immigration policy. There would be no reason to favor one group of outsiders over another; all comers would be welcome. But even liberal philosophers, or most of them, recognize the value of particular obligations in the lives of individuals: some people mean more to me, require more of me, than others. And most of the rest of us, nonphilosophers, believe that collectives, like nation-states, can also be obligated to some people more than to others—as Israel is to Diaspora Jewry and as Palestine would be to its diaspora.

These particular obligations begin with the relatives of citizens. Family reunion is a common feature of immigration policy, although laws differ as to how far the family extends: Does it reach from spouses, children, and parents to in-laws, aunts and uncles, first, second, and third cousins? The further extensions make for what is called (by its critics) "chain" migration. Given the mathematical work on "degrees of separation," we can assume that the chains have no end. Each family claimant has relatives who have relatives of their own, who have relatives, and so on. So states can and do set limits on the relationships they recognize.

Still, the obligation is real: citizens have a claim on their state that it permit the reunion of separated family members. This is an example of legitimate discrimination. There may be people in greater need than this sister of an American citizen, and her husband, her children, and her in-laws, but these people, some of them at least, come first. The state rightly recognizes and endorses the importance of the family.

The obligation to national or ethnic kin may also be subject to limits of one sort or another, but it is from the beginning an extended commitment—and it, too, is widely recognized. When the Soviet Union collapsed, for example, the Finns brought in thousands of Russo-Finns who might have been in trouble in a Russian nation-state and put them on a fast road to citizenship. This was another example of discrimination; there were probably a lot of other people who were going to be in trouble in the new Russia. But I think that the Finns were right to recognize a special obligation to fellow Finns. That might not be the end of their obligations, but it was a legitimate place to start. There are many other examples of this kind of discrimination: Greece taking in the Anatolian Greeks after the establishment of the modern Turkish state, West Germany taking in the east Prussian and Sudetenland Germans after World War II, and Israel's enactment of a Law of Return—probably the most discussed and criticized example of a common policy.

It is an entirely different story, however, when states extend citizenship to fellow nationals living in other countries, as Hungary has done for over one million ethnic Hungarians whose ancestors lived long ago in Greater Hungary. These new citizens are now entitled to vote in Hungarian elections even though the central issues in local politics—taxation, welfare, education, justice—are not issues for them. The outside-Hungary citizens tend to support far-right nationalist parties; their votes affirm the idea that the state doesn't belong only to its inhabitants, who share a common life, but also to an ethnic diaspora. This kind of nationalism violates the most basic principle of democratic politics: that self-government is the work of the governed. In contrast, although Israel is often called the state of the Jewish people, it is in fact the state of its inhabitants, who alone vote in its elections. Diaspora Jews are not enfranchised.

Another example of legitimate partiality in the distribution of citizenship has to do with ideological kinship—and once again Hungarians provide a useful example. The obligation in this case crosses national and ethnic lines. After the Hungarian Revolution of 1956, repressed by Russian troops, thousands of refugees were allowed to enter Great Britain and stay on. I was studying in Britain that year and was amazed to find London suddenly full of Hungarians. In the context of the Cold War, these were friends of the Western democracies, and Britain was one of the leading democracies, hence the obligation, which certainly extended to the United States.

But suppose the revolution had triumphed, the communist regime had been overthrown, and the refugees were former state officials and members of the secret police. I doubt that Britain would have felt any obligation to take them in. The Soviet Union would have been obligated to, assuming that the refugees wanted to go there. In Russia, unlike in Great Britain, they were ideological kin. (It is good to remember that after the Hungarian Revolution of 1848, which also failed, refugees were welcomed in Britain and the United States. The exiled revolutionary leader, Lajos Kossuth, toured America, was formally received by Secretary of State Daniel Webster, and was greeted everywhere by enthusiastic crowds—a nice example of liberal internationalism.)

Taking in familial, ethnic, and ideological kin is a liberal immigration policy. Liberal nationalists would have to insist that it is also necessary to make room for asylum seekers and refugees. If there are too many of these for any one country to take in, it will be necessary to negotiate with the leaders of other countries and to divide and share the burden—an internationalist project. Liberals would add these universal obligations to their particular obligations. It is the combination that justifies the adjective and distinguishes liberal nationalists from nationalists simply, who recognize only the particular obligations, and from cosmopolitans, who recognize only the universal ones.

The adjective "liberal" doesn't only accommodate the interests of existing and aspiring nations; it also recognizes the rights of minorities within the states that nations create. Most nation-states include ethnic and religious minorities, the inclusion determined by ancient conquests, frequently revised borders, and immigration. The liberalism of all such states is tested by their treatment of these groups. Do minority members have the same rights and obligations as all other citizens? Do they have the same economic opportunities? If they are regionally concentrated, do they have a degree of political or cultural autonomy that fits their history and current condition? Are federal arrangements worked out democratically? Consider Canada's asymmetric federalism, which grants greater rights to French-speaking Quebec than to the other provinces: this is the democratic and collaborative work of an assertive minority and a liberal nation.

The liberal qualification of nationalism in general, which makes for the plurality of nations, is paralleled by the liberal qualification of

each particular nationalism. Liberal nations are not created and defined by "blood and soil" or by divine appointment or by a history
that starts at the beginning of time and is never interrupted. The
blood is always mixed; the geography changes over the years; God
isn't involved; and the history is entangled with other histories. The
national story is part true, part imagined, and revisionist historians
periodically challenge the going version.

Minorities in a nation-state, if they are equal citizens, and if the
national culture is in fact open to revision, will tend over time to become fellow nationals. They will make the national language their
first language, the public language of citizenship, and they will fit
themselves into the (newest versions of) national history—as immigrants in France do when they celebrate on Bastille Day a revolution
in which their ancestors had no part. The immigrants often go on to
invoke the principles of that revolution in their struggle for political
equality. At the same time, they, or many of them, work hard to sustain their own cultures and traditions—their second language. Liberal
nationalism allows for what might be called "soft" multiculturalism,
whose manners are described by Jonathan Sachs, the late chief rabbi
of Anglo-Jewry, speaking to his fellow Jews: "If we are to achieve integration without assimilation, it is important to give each of these
[two] languages its due." All the British minorities need to reflect on
what holds them together, on their shared citizenship, and learn to
live alongside radically different men and women. We must "restrain
ourselves," Sachs said, in order "to leave space for the others." Liberal
nationalism needs, and therefore needs to encourage, liberal ethnici-
ties and liberal religions among its minority citizens.

Liberal nations are also ideologically pluralist; their members are
monarchists and republicans, libertarians and socialists, conservatives
and radicals. A multinational, multiracial, multireligious country like

the United States is, by contrast, defined by its politics, and people who reject that politics are called "un-American"—as members of the Communist Party were in the 1950s. "But in a society where social cohesion is based on national, cultural, and historical criteria," Tamir writes, "holding nonconformist views does not necessarily lead to excommunication." Right-wing French politicians do not accuse French communists of engaging in un-French activities. Nor did de Gaulle ever doubt that Jean-Paul Sartre was a respected member of the French nation. Illiberal nationalists in nation-states like France or, in recent years, Poland and Hungary will focus their fiercest hostility on foreigners, or recent Muslim immigrants, or distinctive minorities—like the Jews and the Roma—rather than on ideological opponents. Left/right, capitalist/anticapitalist politics is serious in countries like these, but it has a different valence than it does in the United States.

Even a nation-state where the members of minority groups are equal citizens, where immigrants are welcome, and where ideology, like faith, is free cannot solve the problems created by illiberal and failed states. Millions of men and women in the world today are denied the protection of the states they live in because of their ethnicity or religion. Millions more live in states whose ruined governments cannot protect anybody or in states beset by civil wars that endanger everybody. Legal and literal statelessness is the underside, the negative corollary, of the modern state system. Without a state, or without an effective state, men and women are without rights, dangerously vulnerable. What Hannah Arendt called "the right to have rights" is really the right to belong somewhere. Rights are the product of political association. What, then, can we do for people who don't have political associates, who are not members of an inclusive, reasonably egalitarian, and competent state?

World citizenship isn't an option, for the world isn't a political place. The creation of new states for stateless peoples, like the Kurds and the Palestinians, would be a partial solution. We could complete the state system for the sake of all those who suffer from its incompleteness. But given the cruelty of many existing states and the exclusions of ultra-nationalism, there would still be too many people without effective rights. The contemporary combination of illiberal nationalism and illiberal or populist democracy (and, often, religious zealotry) is a particular threat both to minorities at home and to stateless refugees coming from abroad. The numbers have already overwhelmed the asylum system established by international law.

Humanitarian intervention to stop massacres and expulsions may be one way of helping these people; political and economic sanctions against cruelty earlier on, before the killing begins, would be better. I can imagine a transnational organization that distributes the burdens of helping abused and persecuted people, both when they are in place and when they are refugees, and that enforces an equitable distribution among all established states. It would not be a global government, but rather an organization that would be authoritative but constrained, able to use force but only in limited ways. Nothing like that is on the horizon, but given the scope of climate change and the migrations it is already producing, the necessity will become more and more urgent. If we don't aim carefully at authority and constraint, we will get something much worse.

What would an American version of liberal nationalism look like? I am not sure that the words apply. A distinct American nation may be in formation, but it isn't here yet; America remains racially, ethnically, and religiously divided—like the old empires, perhaps, but not like a standard nation-state. Americans' pride in their democratic institutions; the belief that the United States represents a *novus ordo seclorum*, a new order for the ages; the commitment to the principles of the Declaration of Independence and the Constitution—all this might best be called patriotism. It has no ethnic content, it doesn't appeal to an ancient history; it is, as Steven Smith argues in a recent book, *Reclaiming Patriotism in an Age of Extremes* (2021), a "creedal" affirmation. And since American reality doesn't live up to the creed, patriotism should lead to social and political criticism.

Nationalism in America isn't patriotic; it calls us back to the politics of the old world. It is less an ideology that sets us apart from foreigners than one that divides us at home. The claim of anti-immigrant nationalists in the early years of the twentieth century that America was a "Nordic" nation is an example of this: the number of non-Nordic Americans was already very large. The argument of those who proclaimed "America First" in 1940 was similarly divisive: only some Americans came first; others definitely did not.

The so-called White nationalists of the Trump era are also defending what would have to be, if it exists at all, a nation inside America, not an American nation. When Horace Kallen, the theorist of cultural pluralism, described America as a "democracy of nationalities," he wasn't arguing like a liberal nationalist for the toleration or the civil rights of ethnic and religious minorities, as he might have done if he had been thinking about minority groups in other countries—like the Polish Jews or the Turkish Armenians of his time. Rather, Kallen was arguing like a patriot, insisting that there was no majority in the United States that could be called upon to tolerate minorities. There was only a pluralism of nationalities, each group (except for the Native Americans) living far from its historical homeland. As I argued earlier, Americans who reject democracy and embrace left- or right-wing authoritarianism are called un-American, but there is no racial, religious, or ethnic identity that can be categorized in that way. We are, all of us, Americans. Our self-determination is not national; it is simply democratic.

But our common citizenship and civil religion notwithstanding, isn't America in fact a White country, where immigrant Irish, Italians, Jews, Latinos, and even Asians are progressively "whitened"—and only Blacks are left out, racially stigmatized? There is a hard truth here, but not the whole truth. Americans are divided politically, religiously, culturally, and regionally, as well as racially. Kallen's radically pluralist America really exists, and it has a long history of crosscutting alliances and conflicts. Racism has been a constant feature of American history, but so, in less central ways, have nativism, anti-Semitism, misogyny, homophobia, and religious hatred.

Let's look now more closely at Trumpian nationalism. The White workers who voted in large numbers for Donald Trump in 2020 are often described as nationalists—or, better, as men and women who have bought into a nationalist politics. But they don't have anything like a national history. They have a class history. Together, many of them fought for the right to organize, and then for higher wages and better working conditions, and then for pensions and health care. The disappearance of the industries in which they worked, the collapse of their unions, their abandonment by neoliberal elites, their new economic vulnerability—these are what shape their politics. It isn't so much a nationalist as a populist politics; it isn't directed against an opposing nation or against un-American groups at home. Its demagogues play with racist, anti-Semitic, and anti-immigrant tropes, which obviously have resonance in America today. But how much resonance is unclear, since small but surprising numbers of Blacks and Latinos voted for Trump, apparently not considering themselves his targets but rather identifying with his populist politics. Those voters aren't racists; their actual enemy, and that of their White allies, is the American elite or, specifically, the indifferent or predatory elites, plutocratic and meritocratic, that make up a significant part of our ruling class. It is certainly true that (many of) our plutocrats and meritocrats are not committed to the Declaration's egalitarianism. Still, they play the democratic game (if only because they usually win), and I would not be inclined to call them un-American. They just aren't the patriots they think they are; they aren't sufficiently tied to their fellow Americans; they don't live by our common creed. Unhappily, the populist politicians who lead the opposition to all the elites, or pretend to, have also forgotten the creedal commitments that make for an American patriotism.

If White nationalist/populist politics is an attack on the inclusiveness of American society, Black nationalism is a response to the greatest failure of American inclusion. Whether Black Americans constitute a nation is something for them to decide. It is a question for what the French writer Ernest Renan called a "daily referendum." How the voting is going today, I don't know; I know still less about how it will go tomorrow. But nationalism is a politics, as the White version demonstrates, that doesn't depend on the actual existence of a nation. Many of us on the political left who remember the Black nationalism of the 1960s remember also the difficulty we had understanding and reacting to it.

The early civil rights movement was the work of a racial minority motivated religiously, and also patriotically, in significant ways. It was loyal to the American creed and demanded citizenship in the American city—the "city on a hill." Young leftists who went to the South, including many American Jews, supported that project; we imagined ourselves part of a White/Black (Black/Jewish) alliance. Our focus was on integration and political equality, and we were committed to the nonviolence championed by Black preachers like Ralph Abernathy and Martin Luther King Jr.

But things moved slowly, and for many young Blacks, Christian pacifism didn't seem like a way of standing up, straight and tall, against American racism. They opted for a politics of Black pride, Black power, and radical self-reliance. White liberals and leftists were asked to leave—or to provide support only from the sidelines, which most of us did. Black power was a form of nationalism, a politics of going it alone, a search for heroism—although in truth the young people who sat in and who marched through Southern towns were heroes from the beginning. The everyday work of Black nationalists was often admirable, but it didn't make political sense. Minorities need allies; they do best for themselves when they are part of a coalition with other groups.

The leading nationalist organization was the Black Panthers. Its members were particularly strong in their commitment to self-reliance. They ran educational programs in Black communities, provided breakfasts for schoolchildren, and organized medical clinics. But they talked as if they were revolutionaries, which was a posture, not a politics. And they paraded with uniforms and guns, thereby providing an excuse for what was a quick and brutal police response. Late in the day, Fred Hampton in Chicago abandoned the go-it-alone strategy and formed alliances with White gangs in the city. J. Edgar Hoover, who hated the Panthers with a peculiar passion, found this especially frightening, and under his direction, the FBI organized, together with local police, a raid on Hampton's apartment that was actually a planned assassination. For the moment, that was the end of the nationalist story.

The huge protests organized by Black Lives Matter after the police murder of George Floyd in 2020 looked a lot like the marches and demonstrations of the 1960s: Black and White together, no uniforms, no guns. The riots and the battles with the police in a few cities seemed to signal a new militancy. But the most striking feature of those months was the number and the size of the demonstrations. Nationalism has probably left its mark on contemporary Black activists; Renan's referendum will decide how significant the mark is. But for the moment, most American Blacks aim, I think, at political equality and economic integration first and then at some version of social, religious, or cultural self-determination. Theirs is a familiar American story—in this case, very much unfinished.

The idea that America is "exceptional" is mostly an ideology of self-congratulation, but America is different. Our heterogeneous society includes more racial, ethnic, and religious groups than almost any other (the old empires and the Soviet Union are historical but not contemporary exceptions), and these American groups are dispersed and intermixed to a degree not found in any other country. *E pluribus unum* is probably too optimistic, but *pluribus,* manyness, is true and truly exceptional. The world, however, is moving more and more in our direction. Wars and civil wars, the breakup of empires and the migrations of people, are creating a new heterogeneity everywhere. And that means that nations everywhere now face the two tests that I described above: they are tested by the nations that come next and by the beleaguered minorities within.

We might think now about a third test—the test of cooperation across borders or, more immediately, the test of federalism, as in Europe today. Liberal nationalists and internationalists built the European Union, a project that aims to combine the self-determination of established nation-states with pan-European governance—the latter represented most clearly by a court enforcing human rights across the union. The combination isn't easy, but if the project is visibly successful over the next decades, we may well see similar federations elsewhere. Federalism might be a way of helping both stateless nations and vulnerable minorities. But success depends on the willingness of the citizens of established states to submit themselves to a transnational court and to live with less than full political and economic sovereignty. That is the test.

Brexit was a bold display of unwillingness, but the vote in the United Kingdom to leave the European Union was close. Roughly a month before the vote, I marched with friends in London in support of remaining in the European Union. It was a huge march, with crowds joining at every corner, and I wondered who these people were. Were they liberal nationalists who wanted to repudiate the often ugly chauvinism of the Brexiteers? Or liberal or socialist internationalists who believed in cooperation across borders? Or Europeans who had already added a new identity to their old one? All three were certainly present, and I would guess that many of the marchers were simultaneously liberal nationalists, internationalists, and Europeans. That wasn't a winning combination in the United Kingdom in 2019, but it's possible that those marchers will win in the long run.

British Europeans or French, German, Italian, or Polish Europeans would not be like Irish or Black or Jewish Americans. They would be liberal nationalists rather than creedal patriots, and they would also be internationalists, which Americans mostly are not (despite our engagements around the world). EU citizens would be jointly responsible for the well-being of all the European nations. The European Union is a different kind of federal union, something new, and it might point to forms of political life different from and maybe better than anything I have described in this chapter.

5

Liberal Communitarians

Communitarianism describes the close connection of a group of people who share a strong commitment to a religion, a culture, or a politics. Like nationalists, they aim to advance the interests of their community, but the emphasis of their commitment is internal; they are focused on the quality or the intensity of their communal life. Civic republicanism is probably the best-known version of communitarianism. Jean-Jacques Rousseau is its prophet, and he is definitely not a liberal. Rousseau describes the ideal citizen—a man (women were not yet included) who is busily engaged in every aspect of the common life and who derives a greater proportion of his happiness from public than from private activities. Citizenship involves a commitment that excludes all others. Secondary associations, churches and political parties above all, are a threat to the integrity of the republic—although, Rousseau says, if there are any such associations, it is better if there are a lot of them so that no single one competes with the republic for the loyalty of its citizens.

The citizens do everything for themselves. They don't elect representatives; they "fly" to the assembly, as Rousseau says; theirs is a direct democracy, without professional politicians. And just as there are no politicians, so there are no professional or mercenary soldiers, but rather an army of citizens. Rousseau even suggested that the corvée of the old regime—enforced labor on the king's highways—be replaced by conscripted labor on the republic's highways. Finally, as I have already noted, older citizens rather than trained teachers should teach in the public schools.

Someone once said that "socialism would take too many evenings." Years ago, I quoted that line and attributed it to Oscar Wilde (it sounded like him). Wilde scholars deny that he ever said it, so it has sometimes been attributed to me. But I am not smart enough. This is one of those blazing sentences that defines a politics. It applies, however, most clearly to civic republicanism, which would also take too many mornings and afternoons. Marx famously described the freedom of life in a communist society: we would hunt in the morning, fish in the afternoon, rear cattle in the evening, and criticize after dinner. He omitted the endless meetings that Rousseau's civic republic would require: we would meet in the morning to argue about which animal species were allowed to the hunters and then, in the afternoon, to discuss the maximum catch for each fisherman or -woman. In the evening, we would debate alternative theses on cattle rearing and then rush through dinner for the criticism to come, which would last long into the night.

Marx's imagery is remarkable given what he wrote about the "idiocy of rural life." In any case, we live in cities now, so let's look at an urban example of citizens doing everything for themselves. Rousseau says nothing about the police, who didn't yet exist in their modern form. But contemporary abolitionists, who argue for replacing the police with neighborhood committees, are his spiritual descendants. Here is a question of immediate relevance: Do we want to be policed not by the police but by our neighbors?

The idea is excitingly radical, but it isn't new. I know something about its history because long ago, when I was a graduate student, I decided to write my doctoral dissertation on the English revolution of the 1640s, the Puritan revolution, which I called the "revolution of the saints." The saints were in favor of neighborhood committees. In John Calvin's Geneva, law and order were maintained through "mutual surveillance." Church members (ideally all Genevans were church members) "watched, investigated, and chastised" each other.

The Puritans carried this discipline to England, where it was enforced in their congregations but not further, since the Holy Commonwealth didn't last long enough to extend "watchfulness" and "brotherly admonition" to the country at large. We can get some idea of what these two meant in congregational life from the Reverend Richard Baxter's report (in *The Holy Commonwealth*, 1659) that in his Kidderminster parish the enforcement of the new moral order was made possible "by the zeal and diligence of the godly people of the place who thirsted after the salvation of their neighbors." Today the "godly people of the place"— the righteous and the politically correct—would rotate through the proposed committees; they wouldn't all be at work all the time. But we should worry about their "zeal and diligence," for they would eagerly report to the committees even when they weren't members.

I recognize the importance of having good neighbors and of being one myself. Nancy Rosenblum has written a smart book about the meaning of neighborliness (*Good Neighbors: The Democracy of Everyday Life in America*, 2016); in it she describes a form of social life that falls short of communal intensity but is crucial to the decencies of everyday existence. There are many things I do together with my neighbors. After a hurricane or a blizzard, we help each other repair our property and our lives; when our children are in school, we discuss their courses and teachers and regularly attend PTA meetings; we join arguments about changing the zoning laws and the garbage collection schedule; we share tools and know-how; we stop and talk on the street. Alongside all this, however, I have a right, at times of my choosing, to be invisible to my neighbors.

Liberal communitarians in the United States would prefer to be watched and admonished not by their neighbors but by men and women in uniform; they want to watch their watchers. They would also want their police to share the values of our democracy. In the United States today, a democratically committed police force would, in contrast to the police we know, treat all citizens equally. It would be fully accountable to civilian review; it would be demilitarized, which means deprived of weapons more suitable to a battlefield than to an American city; and it would be trained to de-escalate conflicts. There would be no criminal or civil immunity if its officers used illegal force. Professional police with a code of conduct and enforceable rules of engagement would fit the lifestyle of a liberal community much better than an informal collection of amateurs and zealots would.

But police in the United States today are overengaged and overarmed. The range and extent of their work needs to be reduced. That includes the laws they enforce, the no-knock raids they conduct, the number of people they stop and search, the number they kill, and the number they arrest. Incarceration on the current American scale is the sign of a deranged society—the very opposite of a national (or any other) community. Changing the drug laws would make a big difference in police work; so would a social democratic housing policy. Adding other professionals, including more teachers, welfare workers, and counselors, to the urban mix; opening clubs, gymnasiums, and parks; creating public works and new jobs—all these would give the police less to do (and smaller budgets would naturally follow).

There is one idea that liberal communitarians might adopt from the civic republican repertoire: a year or two of national service for young people in their late teens. They would be conscripted but allowed to choose among many different socially useful tasks. Cooking and cleaning in the nation's prisons could be one of them—work that would help to create a constituency for ending mass incarceration.

Giving everyone a sense of menial but essential work might also reduce the "insolence" of future meritocrats. Here is an egalitarian and communitarian project that doesn't mobilize amateurs and zealots, just the energy and idealism of the young.

The body of citizens is bound to include amateurs and zealots but also everyone else. Citizenship itself is a universal calling, in contrast to roadwork, teaching, and policing—in contrast, also, to all the particular engagements of civil society and especially to party and movement politics. I have made this point before in my discussion of participatory democracy, which is indeed what civic republicanism would require: all the citizens active all the time in the political community. By contrast, in what we might call real politics, there are other communities—parties and movements, for example—whose active members are an important subgroup of the citizens.

Some of these civil society activists are political militants who share not only the history and culture of the republic but also a more particular ideology and a very particular set of emotions: solidarity and hostility. One of the hardest things to teach new activists is how to live with degrees of antagonism that they have never experienced before. They are collectively engaged in an adversarial politics; they are comrades (whether or not they use the word), and some of their fellow citizens are enemies or, at least, opponents. The militants are used to all this; they are also more familiar with ideological argument and more willing to devote full time to the movement, which they are also likely to lead and sometimes dominate.

What I remember most from my movement days are the long hours spent in meetings with friends and allies who wouldn't necessarily be friends or allies in more ordinary times. Some of us were more engaged than others, virtual full-timers, but everyone's involvement was more intense and more narrowly focused than you would find among the citizens of a democratic state. You might say that civic republicanism demands a level of activism more appropriate to a movement than to the political life of the city. This version of communitarianism tries to turn the state into a movement, which it can never be—should never be.

Even in a movement, it is sometimes necessary to worry about the militants. The anti–Vietnam War politics of the late 1960s provides a telling example. In 1967, a small band of teachers and students at Harvard, some of us veterans of Students for a Democratic Society (SDS), organized the Cambridge Neighborhood Committee on Vietnam. Our program: community organizing against the war. Our young and very earnest militants knocked on doors across the city, looking for sympathetic households where we could organize block meetings and urge our neighbors to oppose the war. With signatures collected at those meetings, we managed to put a question on the city ballot—a referendum on the war. Come November, some 40 percent of the voters voted with us against the war. A moral victory? After all, a war in progress is hard to oppose. But we lost badly in every working-class district in the city. We leftists, many of us still believers in the centrality of the class struggle, carried with us only the bourgeoisie of Harvard Square and its surround. What happened?

The answer is easy and sad. The young militants who went door to door were exempt from the draft because they were in college, and they were talking to people whose sons and daughters were in Vietnam. They must have come across as naïve, smug, or arrogant. It had never occurred to us that to do community organizing you needed to know something about the community. Ideological certainty wasn't enough. You had to approach your neighbors with sympathy and understanding. Perhaps that is what communitarianism means—or should mean. Against our will, we antiwar activists produced a pro-war reaction among many of our neighbors: these were some of the people who came to be called Reagan Democrats, working-class men and women who moved to the right in the course of the next decade.

The civic republic of Rousseau's *Social Contract* is also an illiberal nation-state, as Rousseau himself makes clear in his programmatic *The Government of Poland*. There he describes the education of future citizens: they are to study Polish history, Polish geography, Polish culture, Polish literature—and nothing else. "It is education that must give souls a national formation, and direct their opinions and tastes in such a way that they will be patriots by inclination, by passion, by necessity." This kind of education would also introduce the students to a much more intense version of civil religion than anything we have seen in liberal democracies, a ritual celebration of Polishness (or Frenchness, or . . .) meant to evoke a strong emotional response. Here communtarianism and nationalism are brought together in a radically illiberal union.

I used to teach Rousseau's politics, and I always felt that his republic was an overheated community where citizenship was turned into a new form of oppression. A liberal communitarianism would reduce the heat. It would allow citizens to avoid (some) meetings for the sake of their private happiness—to watch a baseball game, go to the movies, play with the children, work in the garden, make love, or just sit with friends, drink coffee, and talk. It would combine the zeal of participatory democracy with the coolness of representative democracy, so that those who don't love politics would still have a say in political decisions. Its schools would aim at creating patriots by inclination but not by necessity. Students would read novels translated from other languages (and also learn the other languages) and study the history, geography, and politics of other countries.

Alternatively, liberal communitarians might avoid the civic republic altogether, arguing that the state should be a liberal democracy or a liberal social democracy that provides a framework for a plurality of communities, some heated and some not. This is my own preferred version of communitarianism. Let there be many communities! Of course, some people will make one community central in their lives, relish its intensity, and set themselves apart from (and perhaps against) their fellow citizens. Identity politics usually follows from a narrow focus on the material interests of the group, but it is aided and abetted by an illiberal communitarianism.

Many of us will choose instead to be members of different communities, and the intensity of our commitment will vary across the plurality of our memberships. This is the life of civil society, which includes not only parties and movements but all the religious, ethnic, economic, philanthropic, and cultural organizations that a liberal democracy encourages, So I can be, all at once, a Jew, a socialist, a *Dissent*-nik, an academic political theorist, a New Yorker, an active (but part-time) citizen of the American republic—and a brother, husband, father, and grandfather.

I think that most Americans have their best experiences of communal work and camaraderie in the associations that their many identities produce—in churches, synagogues, and mosques, in unions, professional groupings, and political clubs, and in extended families. These are the places for close, intense, personal relationships. Here is where we talk, argue, negotiate, come together. Here is the social space for ritual enactments, memorial celebrations, displays of solidarity, and mutual recognition. But these distinct and separate activities and performances don't necessarily separate us from each other, and that is precisely because we participate in so many of them, across so many associational lines. Even people who choose a religious, racial, ethnic, or gendered version of identity are still likely to participate in local politics along with neighbors who identify differently; they are still likely to support an inclusive, "big tent" political party, celebrate Memorial Day and the Fourth of July, and vote in local and national elections. They still imagine themselves as citizens of the republic. They are all still in the same boat.

But there are "greedy" associations, as my Brandeis teacher Lewis Coser called them, associations that make radical and exclusive claims on their members' emotions and on their everyday commitments. The political or religious sect is the best example of this; it is the one that Coser first wrote about in *Dissent* after he and his comrades left sectarianism behind and the one that I wrote about when describing the origins of the magazine. Let us consider the sect as a community that takes shape when some group of people with a new doctrine or an urgent message face political or religious defeat or when prospects for any kind of significant support are dim. Hoping that their time will come, they aim at survival by hardening the doctrine and imposing a tight discipline on their members. They create a walled community of true believers, and they produce an exaggerated version of Rousseau's "greater happiness from public than from private activities." The life of the sect merges the public and the private; it is the whole life of those who share it, and they, I suppose, find some kind of happiness there.

Sects are not democratic; there usually is a charismatic leader of some kind who knows all the religiously or politically correct doctrines and provides the day-to-day applications. If disagreement arises, the most likely outcome is a split and the appearance of a new sect with a new leader who proclaims a corrected set of doctrines. Protestantism in religion produced many churches, and Marxism in politics produced many parties, all of them operating within civil society in competition with other churches and parties—and also a large number of sects that lived radically apart. Think of sectaries as endlessly protesting Protestants and endlessly marxizing Marxists.

They live in greedy communities that most of us would never want to inhabit.

In chapter 2 I described civil society as a world of voluntary associations. Perhaps the most profound lesson of communitarianism is that not all membership is voluntary. People do choose to join religious and political sects. The Protestant Reformation introduced the "gathered" congregation, which is the dominant form of religious life in the United States today. Similarly, we join (and leave) political parties and social movements. But nationality and religion are not choices for most people. The citizens of Rousseau's civic republic are, mostly, born members, as are the citizens of every political community. I never chose to be an American or a Jew—certainly not in the same way that I chose to be a member of the Democratic Party, the American Political Science Association, or the Society for the Elimination of Lousy Philosophy.

We can swear allegiance to another country, and we can convert to another religion or abandon religion entirely. But national and religious connections are very hard to break, and it is only a minority of men and women who actually break away. The inner life of involuntary associations is not necessarily intense, although there commonly is a core of members for whom belonging is central to their self-understanding (their identity). But even for the others, it is difficult to consciously reject what they never consciously accepted. They simply are what they are. How should liberal communitarians feel about that?

As in my other cases, the commitment is carried by the noun. I am a communitarian insofar as I value the bondedness and mutuality of communal life. I want to belong somewhere (or in several somewheres). Protagonists of the adjective "liberal" would qualify the commitment, allow for degrees of bondedness and mutuality, make it possible for me to reject or evade the greediness of some communities, insist that there are different ways of being an American and a Jew. By contrast, libertarian individualists and cosmopolitan philosophers would want to escape from any kind of communal life. Or they would endorse a more casual view of membership and a minimalist view of the obligations it entails. The adjective "liberal" is compatible with something stronger than that—even as it resists the tyranny of all-out participation.

6

Liberal Feminists

Of course men can be feminists, and these days many are and are eager to tell us so. My wife is a bolshevik feminist who never let me open a door for her, or help her on with her coat, or pay for her movie ticket when we were dating—as the conventions of those ancient days required. We have two daughters and a granddaughter who were born feminists. My sister is a lifelong feminist. And I want a world as open to all of them as to any man. There must be millions of husbands, fathers, brothers, and grandfathers like that: call it family feminism. It is too easy.

At Harvard in 1970, I was appointed co-chair, along with the medieval historian Caroline Bynum, of a committee on the status of women at the university. In those years, the late 1960s and early 1970s, there was a group of women graduate students enrolled in the Government Department, where I taught, who were smart, tough, and ambitious—and I wanted a world as open to them as to any male student. Professor Bynum and I wrote a report with twenty-four proposals aimed at beginning, nothing more, to open the university. The situation was so bad that we had no difficulty coming up with twenty-four necessary reforms: more appointments of women to the faculty, greater flexibility in work and work schedules, extended maternity leave, extra time until tenure consideration for new mothers, equal access to all university services, day care added to those services, birth control advice and support at the Health Center, and much more.

The faculty voted for only the first of our proposals, urging departments to hire more women, and ignored or postponed the rest. It was many years before some of the others were adopted. We were well ahead of our time, and I am grateful to my co-chair for keeping me up to speed. Still, liberal and leftist professors jumped to express their support. Faculty feminism is also too easy.

If you really want to be a feminist, you have to join the arguments about what feminism means, and if you are a male outsider, you need helpers from the inside. After the women related to me and after Caroline Bynum, my most important helper was Susan Moller Okin, a graduate student from New Zealand, who wanted to write a feminist history of Western political thought as her doctoral dissertation. Some faculty members thought that was too ambitious a project for someone so young. But I believed that Okin could do it and supported her and protected her as she sat rereading Plato, Aristotle, Hobbes, Rousseau, and all the rest from a radically new perspective. I am sure that I learned more from our meetings than she did. The book that followed the dissertation was called *Women in Western Political Thought* (1979), and it was pathbreaking.

Okin's second book, *Justice, Gender, and the Family* (1989), was a critique of contemporary theories of social justice, mine among them. She was as sharp with current books as she had been with canonical books, but she wrote about my *Spheres of Justice* with what I can only call liberal generosity—which didn't diminish the force of her critique. She was indeed a liberal feminist, one of the best representatives of that kind of politics in recent decades. At a time when many of her sisters were fiercely antiliberal, she defended the Enlightenment. "Liberalism properly understood," she wrote, "with its radical refusal to accept hierarchy and its focus on the freedom and equality of individuals, is crucial to feminism."

Okin was a key protagonist in two of the most important arguments about feminist politics; she is best known for her emphasis on justice in the family and her critique of multiculturalism. I will write about both—and also about the men and women who disagreed with her. The "just family" was challenged mostly by male communitarians defending intimacy, and the critique of multiculturalism was challenged mostly by female communitarians (who may not have called themselves that) defending the "politics of difference." I am simplifying here and will continue to do so. Be careful; it's a minefield.

The patriarchal family was, for obvious reasons, the first object of feminist attack, with some writers favoring abolition and some, like Okin, favoring egalitarian reform. The common response from male sympathizers was to change the subject and talk about extra-familial discrimination. "Liberation begins outside," I wrote in 1983. Open the economy at all levels, fund daycare and require paid maternity leave, break the glass ceiling, bring women into professional positions, encourage them to run for public office—and then family relations would necessarily change. (They have indeed changed, but nowhere near as much as we predicted.) Communitarian writers joined the argument, insisting that the intimacy of the family, the original community, could not be reformed by political interventions in the name of justice. Women are not a group like Blacks or Jews, historically segregated and confined in a ghetto. They aren't a minority; they live among men, who are their fathers, brothers, husbands, lovers, sons, and friends, and in relationships that are shaped by tradition, custom, and personal negotiation—only secondarily and dangerously by state law.

You could say that the defense of the family against state intervention was the original liberal project—as in the old maxim "A man's home is his castle." But in the beginning the maxim captured the complacency of aristocratic men whose castles were their homes, where they ruled like kings, and then it was the maxim of men generally, who hoped to rule like kings. We have to consider the idea that the subordination of women begins in castles and homes, begins in the patriarchal family, not outside it, and that discrimination in the larger society is an extension of what has gone on for centuries domestically. If that is so, then some kind of state intervention would seem to be a necessary remedy.

Consider an extreme case: in 1829, the British banned the suttee—the self-immolation of a Hindu widow on her husband's funeral pyre—in the Indian states that they controlled. For many years before that, the East India Company and then the British government had tolerated the practice because of what a mid-twentieth-century historian, Sir Percival Griffiths, calls their "declared intention of respecting both Hindu and Muslim beliefs and allowing the free exercise of religious rights." "Free exercise" certainly sounds like a liberal position. But the women were often coerced by their male relatives— I would guess almost always coerced—so their right to life and liberty was surely in question. I agree that the British should not have been in India in the first place. Yet they were there, they were in charge, and they were right finally to stop the widows' suicides despite their source in religious belief.

The suttee would not be tolerated here at home, but what about less extreme family practices? Should the liberal democratic state insist on the equal treatment of women in groups that are religiously or culturally committed to unequal treatment? Should liberal feminists support the use of state power to transform gender relations more broadly?

Here the argument about the family connects with the argument that was begun by Okin's brave and controversial article "Is Multi-Culturalism Bad for Women?" Her answer was yes, it is whenever multiculturalism involves, as its harder versions do, the toleration, accommodation, or defense of misogynistic practices in religious or ethnic groups. That sounds like an accurate description of at least some versions of the "politics of difference." Liberal feminists go on to argue that even though the democratic state has to tolerate the different religious and ethnic groups, it also has to set limits on their practices. Balancing toleration and constraint is what the adjective "liberal" requires. The limits would be shaped by—Okin's words—the "rejection of hierarchy and [the] focus on the freedom and equality of individuals."

We will need to distinguish among different degrees of misogyny and different types of state intervention. And, of course, we have to listen to the women involved—the ones we liberal feminists think of as victims, who may not have that view of themselves. Their voices are not determinative, however, at least not entirely and not always. I don't say that because I think that ultra-Orthodox Jewish women who support the patriarchal regime or women living under Islamist rule who praise their rulers are suffering from "false consciousness"—a doctrine that should make liberal democrats and liberal feminists uneasy. "Consciousness raising" was an early feminist project, and I am told that it worked best when the women involved respected each other's religious beliefs and life experiences. Liberal feminists, especially, would recognize and build on the myriad ways in which women coped with, evaded, mocked, and resisted male domination even while remaining within the patriarchal community They had reasons for remaining, which had to do with beliefs, traditions, solidarity, and security. But—and this is the crucial point—those reasons are not sufficient to determine the policies that their fellow citizens should support or that the state they inhabit should enforce.

The advocates of a hard multiculturalism commonly claim to be defending women against colonial-minded and westernizing elites eager to use state power to promote eighteenth-century Enlightenment ideals. The claim has merit, but so does the project it condemns. I think of it now as a domestic project; I don't believe that liberal feminists would support the use of state or military power to enforce Enlightenment ideals around the world. But if religious or ethnic groups come—as migrants, refugees, or asylum seekers—to live in a country whose common life and political arrangements have been shaped by those ideals, their members will have to adjust, to some degree, in some ways, to what they find. Yes, the ideals are subject to ongoing revision, and adjustments will be required by the locals as well as by the newcomers. These twin processes will produce a new politics of difference, but one that isn't achieved at the expense of women's rights.

How much can the liberal democratic state insist on when it defends those rights? My answer to that question probably applies also to Indigenous peoples whose laws and customs are patriarchal, as in many Native American tribes. Their members were conquered, massacred, and dispossessed in the past, so reparations are due them, not cultural correction. Still, they have no legal or moral right to oppress women.

The state's role is limited, but it is also necessary, especially in the case of the young, the country's future citizens. The state should, for example, prevent early and forced marriages, treat honor killings as murder, punish brutal acts against girls and women within the family, and ban the more extreme forms of genital cutting—but not the more minor forms, given that male circumcision is (rightly) allowed. All this is required in the name of individual rights. The state can also insist on the education of both boys and girls and require that they be taught civics and American history even in privately run religious schools committed to a different curriculum. Public schools can go further. They can make sure that students study the history and sociology of the family and learn something about the many possible familial arrangements. The country's children, all of them, have to be prepared to coexist with people different from themselves and to participate in democratic politics.

Interventions of these kinds leave room for cultural difference, but a democratic and egalitarian citizenship does test the robustness of particular religious and ethnic groups. That's fair enough. If the group can't survive such state interventions, maybe it shouldn't survive. That's a hard thing to say, but easier for me since, as a liberal communitarian (and a liberal Jew), I have confidence in cultural robustness. Women have always played a major role in sustaining cultural life. A raised consciousness won't necessarily lead them to abandon that role; perhaps, instead, they will be even more engaged, since the culture they sustain will now include them in new ways.

But how should we respond if the women involved, especially now the older women, defend the old ways? Let's say, although I doubt it is true, that they fully accept what we think is unacceptable: wife beating, forced seclusion, and legal dependency, all part of the basic patriarchal regime. I should be careful here. Recently I came across a legal responsa written by a medieval rabbi about a man charged with beating his wife. "I never heard of such a thing," the rabbi wrote. His denial is comic, but we do have to consider how earlier generations of men and women regarded a practice that seems obviously wrong today. State interventions must be keyed to the felt realities of patriarchal rule; it will always be necessary to study the realities. Still, a liberal state will work hard to end wife beating, forced seclusion, and legal dependency.

There is one case where state officials must be cautious. When cultural groups, like the Native Americans, have been conquered and oppressed, or are currently under attack, many women will choose solidarity over equality, their people over their gender—even if they recognize the disadvantages of their gender and even if they experience those disadvantages in, say, the tribal courts. They will stand with their men against external hostility and persecution. The first response of a liberal democracy should be to end the persecution, stop the attacks, and strengthen the social and economic position of the groups. Until all that is well along, interventions should probably be limited, aiming only to prevent the most terrible injuries inflicted by dominant men.

The family is not a sacred place. Overt violence against women and girls should be stopped—by the agents of the state if necessary and even in violation of customary norms. There are, however, practices required by some religious or ethnic cultures that liberal feminists might strongly oppose but still want a liberal democratic state to tolerate. The practices that we need to discuss involve religious hierarchies and dress codes.

In the Roman Catholic Church, women are excluded from the priesthood. Among Orthodox Jews, women are excluded from the rabbinate. Among ultra-Orthodox (Haredi) Jews, they are also excluded from the study of religious law and therefore from any role in the legal life of the community. They are judged but they cannot judge, and the religious courts in which they are judged are given some (limited) standing in American law. But still, this is America; the church, the synagogue, and even the ultra-Orthodox community are, at least in principle, voluntary associations. Women can and do leave the church; they can and do leave Orthodox congregations, and, although this is much harder, they can and sometimes do break away from the Haredi world. Equally important, they can, again in principle, organize inside their communities and work to change the arrangements that disadvantage them. Work of that sort is more and more common.

Should toleration in cases like these include strong measures—as when the state grants tax exemptions to religious organizations like the Catholic Church that exclude women from their top positions? Okin thought not; she opposed the exemptions; I am not sure. Perhaps we should poll the women involved, who are often engaged (men, too) in educational and charitable activities that the exemptions fund.

Large numbers of religious women, in the United States and around the world, are now actively opposing discrimination from inside their community, searching in their sacred texts to find new arguments for gender equality. Committed to different religions, they will produce different versions of feminism, different ways of being liberated women. Only illiberal feminists would argue that there is only one way. The state should certainly not be enlisted as a defender of singularity. Difference is still a value, but it is most valuable when it is produced by women themselves. Whenever they struggle against cultural or religious subordination, state officials should do no more than defend the democratic rights that make the struggle possible.

Internal opposition to hierarchal elites is difficult, even hazardous. But these are battles that the women have to win on their own, which is also, I think, the way they see things. Perhaps the educational interventions that I defended earlier are an example of—I am not sure this is the right term—official helpfulness. The more young women learn about democratic politics, the more the religious hierarchy is at risk, which is as it should be. A good democratic education should put all authoritarian arrangements, religious and secular alike, at risk.

Informal gender hierarchies exist everywhere in civil society, even in liberal and leftist organizations committed to an egalitarian politics. This was famously true of 1960s groups like the Student Nonviolent Coordinating Committee (SNCC) and the Students for a

Democratic Society (SDS)—two organizations run emphatically by men. At *Dissent* magazine, too, the founding editors were men, the members of the editorial board were almost entirely men, something like 90 percent of our writers were men, and the women closest to the magazine were managers, organizers, and helpers of different sorts. There just weren't many women writing about left politics—so the story went. All that changed with the passing of the old guard. When the new editors (still men) looked for women writers—behold, they were there. Not all the women who were there were liberal socialists and liberal feminists, of course, but those were the ones most ready to write for *Dissent.* Soon they filled our pages, and gradually they were invited to join the editorial board and then to bring in more socialist women.

Changes of the same sort must be waiting to happen, even without state support, in all the religious organizations that exclude women from leadership positions. Catholics and Orthodox Jews will one day discover, as liberal Jews already have, that there are large numbers of talented and learned women more than ready to be priests and rabbis.

Some religions impose dress codes on both men and women, but it is the codes for women that are most controversial—for the women themselves and for political militants of different sorts, some friendly, some hostile, to the religions involved. The codes seem to be designed, they are designed, to restrict the freedom of women outside the family and to reinforce the restrictions that exist inside the family. But large numbers of religious women in all the liberal democracies dress as they please, and efforts to ban particular items of clothing, headscarves in France, for example, seem only to increase the number of women who choose to wear whatever is banned—more likely out of solidarity rather than belief. More laws mean more headscarves, more covered bodies. The women are asserting their connection and sympathy with traditionalist relatives, mothers or grandmothers, say, who dress in accordance with the religious codes. Or they are affirming their Muslim identity in the face of what they take to be efforts to target and stigmatize their religion. Or both.

The claim that young girls are forced by their families to respect the codes is true in some cases, probably in many cases. It goes to the heart of Okin's critique of multiculturalism. But I doubt that this is a good place for state intervention. In the long run, familial coercion, just like official coercion, is more likely to inspire defiance than obedience. This is another battle that women should fight for themselves.

But I have to consider one possible exception: religious clothing that covers the face, like the Muslim burqa in its fullest version. Human social life is lived face-to-face; it has been that way since we lived in caves. The erasure of the face, then, means radical social exclusion. It also hides women from legal authorities, hence the insistence on naked faces in official settings—passport offices, welfare agencies, courts—and I think there is justification for that. What should we say about public places generally? There is a lovely passage in *Reading Lolita in Teheran* (2003) where the author, Azar Nafisi, describes the young women who studied prohibited literature, privately and secretly, in her home. "I could not get over the shock of seeing them shed their mandatory veils and robes and burst into color. . . . Gradually each one gained an outline and a shape, becoming her own inimitable self." In a liberal democracy, we would want everyone's inimitable self freely displayed in public as well as in private settings. That probably doesn't mean banning the burqa, just making sure that women are able to shed it whenever they want to.

Schools and universities may be something like government offices, where what is going on requires face-to-face encounters. I once taught a class where several of the students were fully covered. I found it unnerving when, after the class, one of the women came up to me with a question, and I did not know if she was one of those who had spoken in class and, if she was, which of the comments I remembered came from her. I suppose that teachers can learn to distinguish the voices of their students; or they can require everyone to wear name tags or introduce themselves every time they speak. Still, burqas make it hard to make contact—surely that's the point of the covering. Maybe it would be right to insist on the exposure of eyes, nose, and mouth (which was the practice in Nafisi's Iran)—just that much—to make conversation easier. That seems to me a legitimate concession to ask from a religious minority that agrees (or is required) to educate its children. On some occasions, at least, we need to be recognizable to each other.

One day our teenage granddaughter said to my wife: "You know, Grandma, it's not a binary; it's a continuum." She was right, of course. I have been discussing women and girls, but that's not the whole story or maybe even the main story. The feminist critique of essentialist conceptions of male and female has had welcome pluralizing effects. The critique was especially liberating for all the people who aren't grouped together at the two ends of the continuum. The space between was larger than many of us thought, as the multiple capital letters indicate: LGBTQ (with more continually added). Some of the denunciations of heteronormativity did not feel liberating to those of us self-identified as male or female. We may have been enacting binarism, but that didn't mean we were intolerantly insisting on it. Liberal feminists won't insist, nor will they assume, that all "normal" people are by definition intolerant. In any case, now that the continuum has been recognized, it is important to make life possible for everyone located anywhere on it.

Expanding possibilities requires a political campaign against laws, favored by some religious groups, that are designed to make life impossible for non-cisgender groups. Multiculturalism is definitely bad for gays and lesbians, many of whom are members of religious communities where they are not welcomed. State action was necessary to make gay marriage possible, and it remains necessary to ban discrimination against gays in employment. Liberal Christians and Jews have supported these interventions, but many orthodox and fundamentalist believers fiercely oppose them—and right-wing politicians have exploited their opposition.

These are not specifically feminist issues—everyone should be involved—but feminist theorists began the debate about sexuality in all its aspects, and their role continues to be central. They are strongly engaged in the current legal and political arguments about transgender people (the T in LGBTQ)—boys and girls, men and women, who find themselves at or near one end of the continuum but believe that they belong at or near the other end. It is possible to move, even from end to end, but there are obstacles along the way. Perhaps the least difficult to overcome (and the only one I shall consider) is the common refusal of many public and private institutions to allow trans people to use the bathroom of their choice for fear of embarrassing "normal" people. Liberal feminists, and liberals generally, have a simple solution, requiring only a small architectural innovation: the reintroduction of doors. State action and private initiative together could easily accomplish a simple liberal purpose: to humiliate no one, to make everyone comfortable and safe.

Since the use of state power is a standard liberal preoccupation, I have focused almost entirely on the role of the state in either tolerating or trying to bar or reform misogynistic (and other intolerant) practices. When is coercive action justified? When should liberals hold back? I have defended a soft multiculturalism, aimed at eliminating all forms of sexual subordination while leaving room for the politics of difference. More precisely, the aim is to make sure, insofar as state action can make anything sure, that multiculturalism is not bad for women (or for anyone anywhere on the continuum).

Women defending themselves have more recently unleashed the power of civil society. The MeToo movement is an effort to use public accusation, shaming, shunning, and ostracism as weapons against men who think themselves entitled to harass and abuse the women they employ. The range of intolerable behavior is wide. A powerful man imposes his own dress code—high heels and short skirts; remarks lewdly on a woman's appearance; touches her as if he is a close relative; hints that career advancement depends on sexual compliance; invites her to accompany him on "business" trips; assaults and rapes her. The state comes in only at the end and not always with energy and resolve. But women have discovered that informal, unofficial weapons such as public accounts and descriptions of their experience can be highly effective. Some powerful men have, rightly, lost jobs, influence, and reputation. Others have changed their behavior.

There are problems here: civil society may not be the best place for *measured* punishment; indeed, some women have resisted any effort to make the punishment fit the crime. Nor does there seem to be any readiness to forgive men who try to repent and reform. MeToo has its liberal and illiberal versions. I acknowledge the problems. Certainly, it is important to make principled distinctions: male behavior, even bad behavior, isn't all the same. Unsure of the right response to the different behaviors, I turned for help to a woman friend, and she suggested the following list: Some predatory men should be brought to court, some should suffer economically and politically, some should suffer socially, and some, more creepy than predatory, just need a good kick in the pants. Liberal feminists will know how to recognize the differences.

7

Liberal Professors and Intellectuals

Professors and intellectuals have a profession or a vocation, not a particular ideology or creed, but the adjective "liberal" readily applies to the men and women I will be writing about here—sometimes as description, sometimes as aspiration, sometimes as critique. In the old days, before the age of specialization, professors and the kind of people we now call intellectuals were (or thought themselves to be) liberal in the oldest sense of the word. They were men, and more rarely women, of leisure. "For leisure does not mean idleness," T. H. Marshall wrote in an essay on professionalism. "It means the freedom to choose your activities according to your own preferences and your own standards of what is best." So professors at the old universities and unemployed scholars, who often had aristocratic patrons, cultivated the liberal arts and conformed to a standard of liberality that I identified earlier as both attractive and premodern. But leisure no longer characterizes academic or intellectual life. Work in our colleges and universities is probably as pressured as any other kind of work. For those hired as adjuncts, temporary fill-ins, or part-time teachers, the life of a gentleman or gentlewoman scholar is a depressing fantasy. Similarly, freelance intellectuals, writing and editing for the political magazines, earn at best a scant living. Still, the work of both groups can be performed in liberal and illiberal ways.

Some professors are also intellectuals. Lewis Coser defines the academic intellectual as someone "who reads books outside his field."

I want to deal with professors more generally, including those who stick to their field, but I will begin with the ones who teach what might be called speculative subjects, where moral, political, or scientific ideas are discussed, where disagreement is constant, and where "intellectuality" beckons. Professors can teach these subjects to encourage or discourage the speculations of their students; they can invite or repress arguments and counterarguments. Teaching involves choices, and professors are tested by the choices they make.

For many years, I taught political theory, a subject that has been controversial since classical times. There are theorists who describe the controversies without taking positions themselves; they are really intellectual historians. But theorists are allowed to take positions; we have a license to defend particular ideologies and political arrangements. I once taught a course called Socialism, which was not a historical account of the doctrine—how it arose, who first articulated it, how it was received—but rather a defense of one version of it (described in chapter 3). I made the best case I could, subject, since I am a liberal professor, to one constraint: that I alert students to the strongest arguments against my own position. That is not something that I would do at a party or a movement rally; it is a professional, not a political obligation.

College administrators have told me stories of students who come into their offices upset, even weeping: they asked a critical question in class or dared to argue against their professor's strenuously professed opinion and were mocked or denounced as ignorant, naïve, or bigoted. It's often leftist professors, self-righteous and ideologically certain, who figure in stories like that. But more conventional professors can be just as dogmatic and intolerant without seeming so, since they are merely saying "what everybody knows." The dominant ideas of any age, Marx wrote, are the ideas of the ruling class. That is not entirely true; our rulers are not usually full of bright ideas. But professors are, and the ideas most likely to take hold first in the academy and then in the world are those that explain and justify the way things are and the powers that be. It is easy to teach those ideas as if they are uncontroversial. The professors who challenge them are the ones who produce controversies. Liberal professors will invite their students to join the arguments, not just to recognize the correct (antiestablishment) ideological position.

In the 1960s, some professors, undoubtedly those who read books outside their field, urged faculties to take collective positions on issues like conscription or the Vietnam War. I thought that only issues of immediate consequence to the academic community, issues of academic freedom, say, were right for faculty position-taking. In all other cases, I argued that we should speak as individuals, as citizens, and sign statements where our university affiliations are listed "for purposes of identification only." We should never act in ways that would lead untenured teachers and vulnerable graduate students to think that they must conform to some ideological standard. Faculties are not political organizations.

A famous historical example suggests otherwise. Meeting in the last years of the sixteenth century, the professors of the University of Salamanca voted that the Spanish conquest of Central America was a violation of natural law. Samuel Johnson, a classic intellectual *avant la lettre,* thought this a great moment in the history of universities: "I love the University of Salamanca, for when the Spaniards were in doubt as to the lawfulness of conquering America, the University of Salamanca gave it as their opinion that it was unlawful." He spoke this, Boswell reports, "with great emotion." He was right, of course— the faculty vote is difficult to criticize—but this noble decision was possible only because the Salamanca professors constituted a corporate body from which theological dissidents were excluded. Spanish Catholics were still burning heretics in the sixteenth century, no doubt in accordance with natural law. The professors who condemned the conquest were brave men but not liberal professors.

Fashion is a feature of political and academic (and intellectual) life almost as much as it is a feature of the clothing industry, which regularly produces new sartorial styles. Sometimes the three go together: revolutionary politics, enlightenment philosophy, and *sans-cullotes.* More often, a new and exciting doctrine suddenly becomes fashionable, or a research method pops up that is guaranteed to uncover the truth. Or maybe a charismatic teacher imparts secret knowledge to passionate disciples. I remember a time when you couldn't publish an article in one of the leading journals of political theory unless it had at least four footnotes to Giorgio Agamben (I am exaggerating, but that's how it felt). And then, suddenly, Agamben was gone.

The defenders of the latest academic fashion are something like the theorists of the socialist vanguard. They possess true doctrine— even when the essential truths they assert, as with some postmodern professors, are, first, that there is no truth and, second, that essentialism is the paramount intellectual sin. Back in the 1950s, positivism, in the form of the collection and analysis of statistical data (even about Supreme Court decisions), was taken by many of my teachers and colleagues to be the only way to produce a political science that was truly scientific. More recently, rational choice is the vanguard doctrine. I acknowledge the value of both, but not the exclusive value of either. Faculty politics often revolves around the efforts of the advocates of the most advanced (read: newest) doctrine to seize control of their departments and hire only people like themselves. In cases where the doctrine is leftist, this is a benign substitute for seizing control of the state. But the effort in all cases is illiberal. Given the long history of disagreement in almost every academic field, departments that merit the adjective "liberal" will be pluralist and inclusive.

I am sure that smart people can do good work inside any philosophical or methodological paradigm, especially if they regard the paradigm with some degree of skepticism but even if they don't. Medieval realists and nominalists did equally good work, as did scholars working within and outside the dominant theological system, and so did laissez-faire economists and Marxists. On the other hand, scholars who kowtow to the powers that be compromise or degrade their scholarship, whoever the powers are.

Liberal professors, especially the intellectuals among them, may also combine paradigms that seem incompatible. This is a very old practice, though more rare today because of the narrowing effects of specialization. Thomas Aquinas brought together Greek philosophy and Christian theology. Maimonides gave us an Aristotelian version of Judaism. There are also contemporary examples—political philosophers who pay close attention to survey research, German critical theorists who learn from the Oxford analytic philosophers. Mixing is good; it reduces the force of fashion and the reigning orthodoxies; it makes room for liberal professors to maneuver—to act like liberal professors.

Morris Raphael Cohen, who taught philosophy at City College in New York, was famous for his Socratic method in the classroom. He hated lecturing because, he said, "No man, no matter how critical, can stand up before a class and refrain from saying more than he knows." Liberal professors, and Cohen was among the best of them, don't pretend to say only what they know; they define themselves by acknowledging that they are reaching beyond their own knowledge—certainly beyond what they know for certain.

Saying more than you know can be dangerous, so liberal professors will support academic freedom even though its chief beneficiaries will often be illiberal professors. But they won't take this freedom, or any other, to be absolute. Physics departments can dismiss a professor who decides one day that the earth is flat. University geologists and biologists can fire a colleague who insists in every class that the world and all its creatures were created a little less than six thousand years ago. A history professor who denies that the Holocaust happened should not be teaching in a university—although he can say what he pleases, just like the flat earther and the creationist, as a citizen.

We allow universities sponsored by religious groups to fire heretical professors; religious freedom trumps academic freedom. But state universities cannot fire professors who criticize state officials or policies or even the state's constitution. Political theorists are as free to defend monarchy as I was to defend socialism. But what about Nazism or racism? The hard cases are the marginal ones, where liberal professors are inclined to bend over backwards in the name of academic freedom.

Consider these two cases (made up, but not far from actual ones). Here is a professor who teaches a standard course in a standard way on intelligence and intelligence testing but who talks about racial equality with a wink and a nod and posts racist rants on his website. And here is another professor who teaches a course on nationalism where she is brutally critical of Zionism but of no other nationalist ideology and who tweets in the tropes of old-fashioned anti-Semitism. In both cases, their colleagues, standing tall for academic freedom or, perhaps, in an athletic display of backbending, vote to give them tenure. After all, they are smart, they publish, and they avoid explicitly noxious indoctrination in the classroom. The administration then steps in, overrules the faculty decision, and denies tenure, claiming to protect students against professors who have crossed the red lines of racism and anti-Semitism, if only in their extracurricular writing. Immediately, there are national campaigns in defense of academic freedom and in favor of tenure for each of the two.

I might or might not join the campaigns, depending on a close account of the professors' classroom behavior. If they harass students who disagree in class, lower their grades, or refuse to write letters of recommendation for them, they should not get tenure. If they stick to their academic subjects and don't present fantasies as facts, if they are just professors professing, whether you and I agree or disagree with what they profess, they are candidates as good as any others. They are protected by the principle that protects all of us.

But another issue is at stake here, one that has to do with faculty responsibility. In both these invented cases, faculty members read whatever the tenure candidate submitted, solicited external reviews, argued among themselves, and voted. Perhaps some of them voted for tenure only in order to avoid controversy, hoping to be rescued by the administration. I don't think those who went with the flow should be rescued. The judgment of faculty members should be respected; their votes should count. If they have made a bad decision to keep a racist or an anti-Semite, they should have to live for the rest of their academic lives with the colleague they have chosen. I acknowledge possible exceptions, but this should be the general rule. Next time, maybe, the professors will think more carefully before they vote. As for the students, they are probably smart enough to detect bigotry or impervious enough to ignore it. They don't need administrative protection.

In recent years professors have been told that they should not say anything that offends their students. This strange injunction has a righteous beginning—when significant numbers of Black students entered de-segregated American colleges and universities and encountered the casual racism of the old professoriate. Many of the students responded with resentment and anger, which was exactly the right response. But somehow in our sentimentalizing culture, anger got changed into a plea for comfort: I'm offended; I'm insulted; my feelings are hurt.

This is a plea that a lot of students can learn to make. Some years ago, a group of Jewish students from a nearby university came to me complaining that the Black Students Association, with the support of faculty advisors (liberal professors?), had invited Louis Farrakhan, famous for his anti-Semitic views, to speak on campus. The Jewish students were offended, hurt. What should they do? I told them that an invitation to Farrakhan was a political act, and they needed to respond in a political way—with some combination of anger, argument, and conciliation. They should look to be respected, not consoled.

Sensitivities encouraged become ever more sensitive. Consider a recent case at one of our universities where a professor asked his history class if the positives of expanding global commerce in the fifteenth and sixteenth centuries outweighed the negatives. Since the negatives included the growing slave trade, the politically correct answer was obvious, and making it a question "offended" some of the students, who complained to the university authorities. According to a recent article in the online magazine *Persuasion,* the authorities found the professor guilty of "bias, discrimination, and harassment."

This sort of thing is not yet pervasive, but it is certainly too common in American higher education. Lectures are cancelled, speakers shouted down, professors reprimanded and disciplined, students harassed by their fellows—all because of "offensive" opinions. Some liberal professors protest each case, as they should, but many others are hiding, self-censoring, reluctant to say anything that might make them a target. They need to tell their colleagues and their students that the academy is a place, and education is a process wherein one's core beliefs and received opinions are routinely challenged—and sometimes the challenges hurt. What is the right response to a professor who, one of his students thinks, underestimates the moral awfulness of the slave trade? Write a carefully researched and strongly argued paper that gets the awfulness right. Join the argument; don't try to repress it.

Arguments about offending and not offending students, challenging and not challenging them, have now reached our high schools. Actually, they began in high schools long ago when the very language of instruction was disputed, as was the place of prayer in the classroom, the teaching of evolution, and much else. But the arguments are different at the high school level because education there is coercive in ways that university education is not. Attendance is required, as are particular courses, in civics, for example, and textbooks and other books are chosen by elected officials (the Pennsylvania State Legislature required me to read Ben Franklin's *Autobiography* in, I think, ninth grade). The officials presumably look for texts that reflect their own views of American history and politics—two subjects now the focus of fierce debates.

Textbooks are written by professors, and we can hope that liberal professors will write books that give teachers room for their own initiatives and that invite students to think critically. State legislatures and school boards can choose the texts; they are public officials acting on behalf of the voting public, but they must not aim at political indoctrination, and they must not try to censor how the teachers teach. Public education, as I argued in chapter 2, is critically important to democratic government, and professional teachers are its agents. They may teach required subjects and required books, but how they teach is a matter for their own decision (within the limits of civility and equal respect). In the classroom they are like professors: academic freedom is necessary for the work they do. They cannot teach truthtelling if the truths they tell are censored. High school classes must be places where talk is free. Liberal teachers will know how to impose the discipline that makes learning possible without repressing the inquiring minds of their teenage students. Elected officials must not try to hobble inquiry.

Liberal professors should treat their students like young adults. What is equally important is the way they treat their younger colleagues—those at the bottom of the university hierarchy. I suppose the hierarchy can be justified if it is organized on the basis of age, university service, and scholarly achievement. But that was never entirely true, and it certainly isn't true today. Universities have created an academic proletariat whose members have no chance or very little chance of climbing up the hierarchal ladder. Junior colleagues have heavy teaching loads; they often teach part-time in several universities; they work with students that the senior professors ignore—and get no credit for any of it. They have little leisure, inadequate benefits, and no security, which leaves them without time or energy for their own research.

Given these conditions, I am inclined to say that liberal professors have to become liberal socialists, defending the poor and the oppressed in their own working world. They should be the partisans of collegiality. Their departments should be places where established professors, the local hierarchs, take on a sufficient share of the common work and make sure that the others do no more than their share, are well paid to do it, —and, of course, are permitted to do it according to their own lights. The academic freedom of the proles has to be at least as important as the academic freedom of the professors.

Are the professors who support the academic proletariat the same professors who encourage disagreement in their classes, resist fashionable orthodoxies, mix intellectual paradigms, take responsibility for decisions about appointments, and defend each other's academic freedom? Probably not. There are different ways of being a liberal (and an illiberal) professor.

Some professors are intellectuals, and in recent decades many intellectuals have found that they can earn a living only by entering the academy. Historically, however, the members of the intelligentsia have stood apart, proudly independent and without institutional salaries. Intellectuals used to live by their wits, sometimes with wealthy patrons, most often without, on the margins of society or in exile, writing for the little magazines and underground newspapers, hoping to produce a book that would sell more than a few copies. What distinguishes true intellectuals, however, isn't their poverty but what Ignazio Silone calls their "critical consciousness." They look at the world with an oppositional eye or at least with an independent eye: they owe nothing to the powers that be. They are, almost professionally, social critics. I hasten to say, given my own political predilections, that they are not necessarily left-wing critics. There is a long tradition of conservative criticism: opposition to whatever is fashionable and new, a dislike of mass culture and democratic demagoguery, a strong defense of hierarchy and respect for authority. Seasoned with a little irony, all this can still be the work of an independent and even, sometimes, a liberal intellectual.

On both left and right, independence and marginality make for a kind of instability. Intellectuals change their minds, some of them rather too often, or they become political partisans, reckless in their partisanship. So intellectual criticism is followed by the criticism of intellectuals. Two classic texts of twentieth-century politics illustrate the second of these activities: Julien Benda's *The Treason of the Intellectuals* (1927) and Czeław Miłosz's *The Captive Mind* (1953). Both these writers are themselves liberal intellectuals writing against the politicization of the intellect and the loss of critical independence.

Benda defends the Enlightenment ideal of universal truth; he thinks of himself as a dissident in the "age of the intellectual organization of political hatreds." Racism, ultra-nationalism, ideological zealotry— all these represent a betrayal of the intellectual vocation. "Disinterestedness" is Benda's alternative, but I don't think that he means to rule out every kind of political commitment, only those that block or compromise moral judgment.

Miłosz, a recent exile from communist Poland when he wrote his book, aims to explain the transformation of many Polish intellectuals from whatever they were before 1945 into resolute or conformist partisans of the Stalinist regime. The switch wasn't only a matter of coercion and cowardice; Miłosz proposes a catalogue of the ways in which seemingly smart men and women trick themselves into ideological submission. Some readers thought the book too kind to the Stalinist intellectuals—as if explanation is necessarily excuse. What Miłosz has actually written is a savage indictment, if not of particular captive minds, then of the captivity itself. In its way, the book is also a plea for dissidence.

Benda and Miłosz teach us what intellectual life should be like. Let me name, in celebration, some groups of intellectuals who exemplify that life and some of their leading members.

- The French philosophes, the enlighteners, of whom Denis Diderot, who edited the *Encylopédie,* is my personal favorite
- The nineteenth-century Russian intelligentsia, whose greatest representative, Alexander Herzen, spent most of his life in exile
- The writers of the New England renaissance, with Henry David Thoreau their own dissident
- The women of the 1848 Seneca Falls Convention, a Quaker-sponsored meeting, one of whose leading organizers was Elizabeth Cady Stanton, a non-Quaker and a superb agitator

- The American abolitionists, a long list of brave men and women, of whom I will single out Frederick Douglass
- The English Fabians, Sidney and Beatrice Webb among them until they went to Russia and became captive minds
- The poets and novelists of the Harlem Renaissance, with Langston Hughes the one I grew up reading
- The Italian antifascists, members of the group Justice and Liberty, whose leader was Carlo Rosselli
- The New York Jewish intellectuals, magazine writers all, who included among their number a few non-Jews like Dwight Mac-Donald, editor of the wonderful journal *Politics*
- The neocon intellectuals, also mostly Jewish, whose conservatism was both strenuously argued and tempered with social democratic concern by writers like Daniel Bell and who produced in the second generation some tough Never Trumpers

Irving Howe, one of the Jewish New Yorkers and a fierce critic of the neocons, provides the best description of the mind of a true intellectual: it is never a captive mind, but "a mind committed yet dispassionate, ready to stand alone, curious, [and] skeptical." Howe goes on: "The banner of critical independence, ragged and torn though it may be, is still the best we have." I think that professors might carry that banner, too, but it belongs especially to liberal intellectuals.

8

Liberal Jews

Pluralism has been a feature of Jewish history for a very long time. Without a state, a territorial base, or an ecclesiastical hierarchy, exilic Jewry was radically decentralized; each Diaspora community was self-governing, at least insofar as the gentile overlords allowed self-government. In a sense, Judaism was congregationalist long before the Protestant Reformation made congregationalism the organizing principle for half of Christendom. Differences in custom and ritual were common across the Diaspora. Until modern times, however, Jews believed in their unity: Knesset Yisrael, the community of Israel, was singular in character, defined by a supposed theological orthodoxy or by an orthodoxy of observance. Dissident groups like the Karaites were marginalized or expelled. Messianic pretenders sometimes left behind cultish groupings, usually short-lived. At any given moment, there were in fact different ways of being Jewish, but the recognition and appreciation of difference that makes a liberal Jew was hardly possible.

The appearance of Reform Jews and secular Jews in the nineteenth century was entirely new. Judaism became a denominational religion quite suddenly, and just as suddenly emancipation in the West made it possible for many Jews to abandon all the denominations and become unaffiliated and nonobservant Jews, identified simply as members of the Jewish people. Among religious Jews, pluralism took on a new form, exemplified in the joke about the Jew who needs two synagogues, the one he goes to and the one he wouldn't set foot in. The adjective "liberal" doesn't fit this Jew, but plurality, however contested, opens the way to liberalism—and also to disputes about who is and who isn't a Jew or a "real" Jew, disputes that liberal Jews would like to avoid.

The question Who is a Jew? has ancient precedents involving Jews forcibly converted to Christianity who wanted to return to the Jewish community. Did they require a second conversion, a formal ceremony, or had they been Jewish all the time? Is a Jew who sins still a Jew, as the ancient maxim stipulates? The question was differently answered, a sign, perhaps, of pluralism to come. Today, that old question is being asked again, raised in a new form by the creation of the State of Israel and by Diaspora denominationalism. The issue now is the "fit" between Jewish pluralism and a modern, formally secular Jewish state. Things are easier in America.

Israel is supposed to be a refuge for Jews from anywhere in the world who want or need to come. The refuge was legally established in 1950 by the Law of Return (which I described and defended in chapter 4). Who does this law cover? Who is a Jew and entitled to return? The official answer, until a recent Supreme Court decision overturned it, was that anyone born to a Jewish mother or converted to Judaism by an Orthodox rabbi in an Orthodox ceremony was officially Jewish. Given the strength of the Orthodox rabbinate, Reform, Conservative, and Reconstructionist conversions (overseen, perhaps, by a woman rabbi!) were not recognized by Israeli officialdom. But what about converts to Christianity or any other religion? Consider the case of Oswald Rufeisen, also known as Brother Daniel. He was born to a Jewish mother, converted to Catholicism during the Second World War, and became a Carmelite monk, but he continued to think of himself as a member of the Jewish people. During the war, before and after his conversion, he was active in the Belorussian resistance and, taking great risks, saved many of his fellow Jews. In 1959 he went to Israel, claiming citizenship under the Law of Return. The Interior Ministry denied his application and a divided Supreme Court eventually confirmed the denial, ruling that someone who converted to another religion was not a Jew in the ordinary sense ("in the common parlance") intended by the law. Justice Cohen, dissenting, took what I consider a liberal view: "the right to return to Israel belongs to any person who declares that he is a Jew . . . and wishes to settle" in what he considers his homeland. Cohen would allow no religious test, which seems right, and the secular or national test, in his view, is met by the wish to live in a Jewish nation-state. Brother Daniel was a national Jew.

The Israeli philosopher Avishai Margalit, in a commentary on the Court's decision written for volume II of *The Jewish Political Tradition* (more about these volumes later), makes what he calls an "outrageous" argument—which I take to be liberal one. Margalit believes that the idea of Israel as a refuge is the only "defensible rationale" for the Law of Return. In the aftermath of the Holocaust, "no person could be turned down by the state of Israel who would have been persecuted [as a Jew] by the Nazis." In other words, Jewishness, for the purpose of the Law of Return, is determined by anti-Semites, by the persecutors of the Jews. (For other purposes, other determinations would apply.) "The long history of Jewish persecution," Margalit writes, "with no sure refuge available anywhere on earth . . . morally requires Israel to offer Jews everywhere an unconditional asylum." Hence there should be no religious tests and no secular tests: like Justice Cohen, Margalit provides a liberal interpretation of the law, but he replaces Cohn's subjective reading with an objective one appropriate to the experience of persecution, which is never a choice. Still, Brother Daniel did choose to come to Israel; he was a Jew in the eyes of the Nazis, and in his own eyes, and, although it matters little, in my eyes and Margalit's.

I grew up in a Reform congregation that coexisted in a small Pennsylvania town with a Conservative congregation and an Orthodox shul, and I went from there to a largely Jewish university (Brandeis), where there were many different kinds of Jews. But I did not grasp the full range of Jewish pluralism until I was on my way, for the first time, to Israel in 1957. Newly married, my wife and I had spent a year in England and then traveled with two friends across Europe to Athens and its port, Piraeus, where we boarded a ship bound for Haifa. We were the only paying passengers. The other passengers were refugees, paid for by the Jewish Agency: Egyptian Jews forced out of Egypt after the 1956 Suez war and Polish Jews leaving Poland after the Gomulka reforms had brought priests back to the state schools. The Egyptians were "traditional" Jews, pre-denominational; the Poles were communists and strongly secular. We became friendly with one of the Poles, who spoke a fluent English. One morning, his nine-year-old son came running; he had watched the Egyptians at morning prayer and exclaimed to his father, "I thought that Jews were people who didn't pray." Indeed, he had been taken out of school when the priests introduced Catholic prayer.

So here were Jews who prayed and Jews who definitely didn't—polar opposites. Neither group had been liberal in their original habitat. Nor would their recognition of each other as Jews qualify them as liberal Jews. The maxim "Even a Jew who sins is still a Jew" is only the bare beginning of liberalism. What counts is the acceptance of difference as a good thing—a valuing of the other's way of being a Jew without any thought of adopting or imitating it.

Liberal Jews are easy to caricature. They are very moderately committed to one way of being Jewish; look benignly, or maybe indifferently, on all the other ways; congratulate themselves on their broad-mindedness; and avoid as much as they can Jews who are more strongly committed. This is a Jewish version of Trilling's complacent liberal. (I must write carefully here: this is close to home.) But I can also imagine liberal Jews as deeply conflicted, self-tortured—recognizing the value of all the ways of being Jewish and unable to choose among them. They move this way and that, waver, curse their indecision. So long as they are engaged in deciding, even though un-decided, they remain liberal Jews.

I don't know what happened to the nine-year-old Polish boy who thought Jews didn't pray. Israel in 1957 would have offered him many possibilities. Perhaps he grew up and became a "traditional" religious Jew, like the Jews he had never seen before; perhaps he joined the more familiar Israeli communists; perhaps he chose, when he could, as I would have done had I been an immigrant rather than a tourist, the Labor Zionists. Any of these choices is compatible with liberal Jewishness; none of them guarantees that the adjective applies.

The Egyptians and the Poles were on their way to a Jewish state where illiberal Jews, Orthodox and ultra-Orthodox, now as then, are eager to use the coercive power of the state to promote their versions of Judaism and where liberal Jews, many of them irreligious, fight to establish and sustain something like a secular state. The prevailing form of Israeli secularism is imperial in origin, adapted from the Ottoman Empire's millet system. The members of each religious community—Jews, Muslims, and Christians of different sorts—are subject to their own religious courts in matters of family law. Among the Ottomans, this system amounted to a liberal acceptance of group difference. But individuals had to belong to the millet of their group, and the millets were unitary. Similarly in Israel today, the Egyptians and the Poles, different as they were in 1957, would have been able to marry and divorce only in the rabbinic courts, where Orthodox rabbis preside and all other Jewish denominations are excluded. Liberal Jews in Israel work, so far unsuccessfully, for the establishment of civil courts and state-appointed judges administering civil law with regard to all family issues. Their success would mean the end of rabbinic power; religious organization would move toward something like what it is in America, where the organizing principle is voluntary association.

Liberal Jews in the United States have been in the forefront of efforts to sustain the secular state established by the Founders. I am one of those liberal Jews, so my description of American secularism will be a kind of endorsement. I know that all the world is not America and that American arrangements and policies often don't travel well—especially when they are delivered by military force. Still, I want to defend American "separationism," the American version (which may be the original version) of a secular state. Both its rigor and the compromises it involves seem especially suitable for religiously diverse countries. Four principles define its rigor; I will describe each of them and then look at the sometimes inconsistent but always practical arrangements, generally supported by liberal Jews, that make separationist politics work.

First, the coercive power of the state cannot be used on behalf of any religion or any religious purpose or program. This is the famous "wall" between church or synagogue and state, which is actually a prohibition of any kind of state intervention in the religious realm. The wall is also meant to prohibit any religious intervention in the political realm, but the two prohibitions are effectively one, since religious interventions always aim at using the state's coercive power. What is ruled out, to take just one example, is the use of tax money to fund religious schools—Catholic parochial schools and Jewish yeshivas chief among them. This prohibition has been contested since the mid-nineteenth century, and it is eroding today, but it is nonetheless a central feature of American separationism. The key compromises have involved funding parochial school programs for disabled children and sometimes, in some places, providing school lunches or student transportation.

At the same time, most states in the United States require that all schools, public and private, teach courses in American history and civics. Religious schools are not exempt; they can teach whatever religious ideas and values are important to their sponsors, but they must also prepare their students for citizenship. It is widely known that some ultra-Orthodox Jewish day schools teach these courses with a wink and a nod—as if to tell students that citizenship isn't what's really important. Liberal Jews would insist on its importance. Classes in history and civics introduce students to the "first language" of the political community.

Although the United States doesn't have an established church, we do have an established state, a constitutional democracy. That state is in principle religiously uninvolved, but it cannot be politically uninvolved. It aims at its own reproduction; it aims to foster democratic competence and participation—and the schools, as I've argued before, are the key place where that is done. But the state's political commitment has a limit that is interestingly parallel to the limit on its religious commitment. It cannot be religiously partisan, and it must be politically nonpartisan. This means, for example, that a political party can win an election and enact its platform into law, but it cannot use state power to turn its platform into a school catechism—as the Communist Party did in the old Soviet Union.

There is, however, a significant compromise with religion at the other end of the life cycle. Visiting a Jewish nursing home near where we live, I was surprised to learn that a large part of its budget is funded by the federal government. Indeed, tax money is used to fund nursing and old-age homes run by all the religious communities. Medicare and Medicaid, our still incomplete version of a national health-care program, function as a kind of voucher system for these institutions. Elderly men and women without sufficient funds of their own can use government money to pay for a religiously comfortable old age. While the American state is not and, in principle again, should not be involved in the religious formation of children, it can provide a religious home for people who are already fully formed.

This first feature of American separationism has special meaning for the Jews. Most importantly, a negative meaning: no persecution, no forced church attendance, no Inquisition, no mandatory rules about costume, and no prohibited professional employment. But the absence of state coercion and of state support for religious coercion has a powerful positive consequence: it creates a realm of freedom that was most beautifully described, early on, by George Washington in his 1790 letter to the Hebrew congregation of Newport, Rhode Island. He told the Newport Jews that they would not be tolerated "as if it was by the indulgence of one class of citizens that another enjoyed the exercise of their inherent natural rights." The Jews would simply enjoy those rights, and each of them, like every American citizen, would "sit safely under his own vine and fig tree, and there shall be none to make them afraid."

The second principal of American separationism is that illiberal groups, as I wrote in the chapter on liberal feminists, are tolerated by the secular state, but only so far. The laws against discrimination, for example, don't prevent the Catholic Church from excluding women from the priesthood or Orthodox and ultra-Orthodox Jews from excluding women not only from the rabbinate but also from the study of religious law. Amish communities are permitted by the Supreme

Court to end the education of their children several years before the legal school-leaving age: the elders argued that the children needed to know only so much, and the Court agreed. US courts have also allowed the use of forbidden drugs in the religious services of some Native American nations. But the most telling example of toleration or, in this case, accommodation is the existence of the ultra-Orthodox (Haredi) village of Kiryat Joel fifty miles north of New York City. How can there be an ultra-Orthodox village, a religious village, in a secular state? Private-property law allowed the creation of an enclave of houses all owned by Haredi Jews, and the state of New York allowed the incorporation of the enclave as a freestanding village—and also, amazingly, as a public school district.

The argument about the school district went all the way to the Supreme Court, which ruled that the "conferral of power upon a group of citizens who share the same faith" is not the same as the "conferral of power upon a religious institution." No Haredi synagogue or yeshiva could run a public school, but a Haredi village can do exactly that—which, given the views of the village's religious (and political) leaders about the education of boys and girls, should be more troubling than the Court recognized.

The third principal is that the civil religion sponsored by the state should be genuinely civil. Its rituals, holidays, and authoritative texts should not reflect or imitate those of any of (what we might call) the real religions. The Fourth of July, Independence Day, is a good example of a purely civil holiday, whose rituals are entirely independent of Christianity, the dominant American religion, as well as independent of all the others. The US Constitution is a similarly good example of a text that has become something like sacred, but only in a civil sense. We consider it immensely valuable but also amendable, as divine law presumably is not. Alexander Hamilton, asked why the

Preamble to the Constitution doesn't mention God, is said to have responded: "We forgot." We might call that a liberal forgetfulness.

But it is hard to avoid religion in the celebration of Memorial Day, when the nation honors the men and women who died in its defense, since for most Americans, for most people everywhere, death is an event that is religiously marked. I remember the moving celebrations of Memorial Day immediately after World War II in the small town where I grew up: everyone walked (we schoolchildren marched) to the cemetery and listened to the celebratory words of a minister, a priest, and a rabbi (today Islam would also be represented); the mayor spoke for the state and perhaps, although he wouldn't have said so, for any atheists present. The Jews were a tiny minority in the town, so the rabbi's appearance was a powerful sign, for us, of acceptance. Pluralism at moments like that supports secularism even when the moment isn't itself secular. All religions are represented; none are endorsed.

The inauguration of an American president has sometimes been taken as an example of the Christian colonization of our public culture. But the presidential oath derives from feudal, not Christian, practice. Reciting poetry on such occasions is a long-established custom, of which the biblical psalms (the "royal" psalms) are an early example. The "address from the throne" is taken over from monarchic regimes, where it is pretty much universal. Only the hand-on-the-Bible is specifically Christian, and American law permits alternatives to that if any president-elect ever wants to make a secularist point.

Like the celebration of Memorial Day, the closing of government offices on Sundays is a pragmatic compromise with, in this case, the majority religion. But it is worth remembering that in 1810, the US Congress voted that mail be delivered seven days a week because the state could not recognize a religious day of rest. Early on in the history of the American republic, it seems, secularism took a radical form. But the radicalism didn't work; at any rate, it was locally and successfully opposed. For decades Sabbatarians managed to enact blue laws in many cities and towns prohibiting anyone, including the post office, from doing business on Sunday. Laws like those were a clear violation of separationist doctrine, and they were strongly opposed by Orthodox Jews, who had already shut down their businesses on Saturday and wanted to reopen on Sunday; they were opposed also, on principle, by liberal Jews and liberal Christians. Blue laws disappeared years ago, but the mail is no longer delivered on Sundays, and no one really objects.

Christmas in America is a harder case; it is often celebrated with state help—as when a crèche is set up in the town square or carols are sung in the public schools. In my hometown, a few principled atheists regularly challenged the legality of the crèche. The Jews were smart enough to keep quiet. Let the Christian majority enjoy some public recognition of one of its holiest days. You might say that we tolerated the crèche; setting it up was certainly not a natural right, but it would have been ungenerous to make a fuss (and also unwise). As for the carols, one Jewish mother told her daughter to sing along if she liked the music. "If her Jewishness is threatened by 'Silent Night,' I haven't done my job." I would call that a liberal response.

The fourth principle of separation requires an acceptance of the open, pragmatic, contingent, uncertain, inconclusive, and tolerant character of all arguments, positions, and alliances on the political side of the line. This is the hardest requirement of the four, since it can never (and should never) be made a matter for legal enforcement. It has to do with democratic political culture and public education. The language of religion is absolutist in character, at least some of the time. It is also, obviously, discursive and speculative (as it already was among Catholic and Jewish Aristotelians in the Middle Ages), But absolutism in the form of faith, mystery, dogma, heresy, and orthodoxy is not alien to religion, whereas it should be alien to politics, at least, to democratic politics, so that members of the *demos* can talk easily to one another. "Whoever doesn't believe in revelation from Sinai will have no place in the world-to-come" is the sort of statement that has no place in political discourse—not its content, clearly, and not its tone either. The principle is this: political language, even when it is spoken fiercely and loudly, should always be open to questioning, disagreement, and revision.

We know that it isn't always open. When politics goes bad, we often use religious language to describe it: the cult of personality, sectarian dogmas, the ritual incantation of the party line, the search for heretics, messianic pretension, and so on. A healthy political competition invites different descriptive terms. Even the language of war—fight a campaign, adopt a strategy, outflank your opponents (on the right or left)—is more compatible with democratic politics than religious discourse is. In war it happens at least sometimes that opposing soldiers respect one another, whereas infidels and apostates haven't been respected in the history of most of the world's religions.

Historically, pretty much every religious orthodoxy has been hostile to democracy, at least in its first confrontation with democratic politics; later on, all sorts of accommodation are possible. In the beginning the case is clear: the word of God and the laws of God are not subject to popular debate and revision. It isn't possible in any ecclesiastical regime to imagine taking turns (rotating) in office with heretics, let alone with infidels. But the idea of taking turns with political opponents is central to democratic politics. As I have already said, no one wants to rotate out of office, but all democratic officeholders, including the most pious among them, accept the risks of rotation.

So people whose views have been religiously formed have to learn, and many have learned, to express them in ways that make sense to irreligious or differently religious fellow citizens. Talk of God's will and appeals to revealed truth are best left out of political discourse. But this, again, isn't an absolutist position in our secular state. Martin Luther King Jr.'s's invocation of the biblical line that describes all human beings as "created in the image of God" seemed to work well in our democratic politics—I have never heard committed atheists objecting. But when I repeat it, I also extend it: "All human beings are created in the image of God, whether or not God exists." I suppose that is a universalizing, if illogical, move, but the original version has proven to be perfectly acceptable. It represents another compromise with or even acceptance of a widely shared—and, for people on the liberal left, politically useful—religious idea. But other religious ideas, the value of life, for example, or care for the poor, have also been successfully invoked in American political discourse.

Secular talk with religious phrases probably works better than secular talk by itself—at least in America. The cultural requirements of separationism don't prohibit religious references in our political discourse so long as religious or any other minorities are not condemned or excluded. "Creation in the image" excludes no one. Nor does the American wall exclude the compromises that I have already mentioned, like Memorial Day religiosity and Sunday observance. The wall isn't an impenetrable barrier; it doesn't prevent occasional crossings. Perhaps we should call this liberal separationism, where the adjective "liberal" works against any sort of absolutism and describes a society as open as it should be. Against any illiberal closure we look for a constitutional remedy.

The secular state favored by liberal Jews can accommodate illiberal Jews, and the understanding of Jewishness favored by liberal Jews includes Jews with every conceivable relation to the Jewish tradition as well as those with no relation at all. Lapsed Catholics are probably not Catholics anymore, but lapsed Jews are Jews still. But there is, as I understand these things, a preferred liberal way of relating to the Jewish tradition. For many years, I have been engaged, with colleagues in Israel, in an effort to work out and exemplify that relationship. Our project is called *The Jewish Political Tradition;* it consists of four volumes of texts and commentaries (the first three already published by Yale University Press) dealing with political life and thought from the Bible, the Talmud, and rabbinic responsa up to and including texts from the modern Diaspora and the new state. Our aim is an appreciative and at the same time a critical reading of the tradition, presented "warts and all," as Oliver Cromwell said he wanted to be painted.

A liberal reading of the tradition could be one that finds all our favorite liberal ideas lurking, as it were, in the old texts: the social contract, limited government, consent of the people, concern for the common good. It is all there if one reads with a knowing eye. But much else is also there. Excluding or ignoring the illiberal moments and the authoritarian arguments that make us uncomfortable isn't liberal but apologetic—or, perhaps, too generous. So as we review the Jewish political tradition we attempt a full-scale engagement. Commentators are urged to read a text or group of texts and ask: Is this right? Is this a good argument? Should we repeat it, revise it, or reject it? We do our best to avoid pious or apologetic commentaries but also arrogant or know-it-all critiques, written as if the biblical writers or the rabbis failed to appreciate the correct ideological position. We are, in our own way, traditional Jews, committed to the continuity of Jewish history and to the arguments that are an essential part of it.

Friends sometimes ask us: "So, what can we learn from the Jewish political tradition?" Our answer takes the form of a rabbinic parable. A French king set his son to studying French political thought. The boy dutifully studied for many months and then reported to his father. "Well," said the king, "what can we learn from the French political tradition?" "Papa," the boy replied, "there are writers defending monarchy, thank heaven, but there are also fierce republicans; there are liberals and conservatives, socialists, communists, and fascists. I couldn't find a single, authoritative teaching." It is the same with the Jewish political tradition: all possible political positions are represented. In our contemporary arguments, textual support is always available. "The devil can cite Scripture for his purpose," Shakespeare wrote. Good people can, too.

The multiplicity of positions means that learning from the Jewish (or the French) political tradition has to be interpretive and argumentative. Consider, for example, the fact that the rabbis disagreed vigorously among themselves and that the editors of the Talmud decided to record the disagreements and preserve the dissenting legal opinions. Surely this points toward, although it isn't the same as, liberal pluralism. You might say that the rabbis were pluralists manqué, without a doctrine, although they wouldn't have been comfortable with that idea. Or consider the long history of exile and persecution, which surely helps to explain why so many Jews today are liberal democrats and liberal socialists, defending the rights of minorities and of the oppressed generally. But I recognize that conservatives and neoconservatives and illiberal democrats and socialists can also find much in the tradition to consider.

Studying the Jewish tradition is one way, the traditional way, of living a Jewish life. Dwelling on the Holocaust and trying to draw meaning from it is another, more recent, and very different way. The Holocaust looms large in Jewish history—how could it not? We Jews have to remember the murder of the six million much as we remember slavery in Egypt. Jews everywhere should imagine themselves among the slaves and among the six million. I think of that as a commandment, and not one that requires individual consent. If I choose to live any kind of Jewish life, I am bound to remember. And with the remembrance comes the hope for freedom and well-being for the Jews—and for all the "others," too. "Do not oppress the stranger; you yourselves know how it feels to be a stranger, because you were strangers in Egypt." But the memories of slavery, persecution, and death can also have a blighting effect on Jewish consciousness.

I am not bound to make those memories the central fact about Jewish existence or the only source of its meaning. Following the historian Salo Baron, I want to avoid becoming "enamored with the tales of ancient and modern persecutions." Baron rejected what he called "the lachrymose conception" of Jewish history—"an overemphasis on Jewish suffering [that] distorted the total picture of Jewish historical evolution." Our history is also a story of bold innovation, intellectual creativity, and against-the-odds collective survival. Without sovereignty or territory, and often without coercive power, we sustained a national existence. There is much to learn, as well as much to remember, from the years of Jewish exile, and even much to celebrate.

We didn't do it all by ourselves. The Passover Haggadah includes a passage that reads like this: "In every generation there are those who rise up against us to annihilate us." In fact, however, there were golden ages, whose generations did not face annihilation. It is also true that in every age Jews found allies: enlightened rulers who protected us (or who could be bribed to protect us), philo-Judaic scholars, men and women eager to trade and invest with us, liberals and democrats who offered us citizenship and opposed every sort of discrimination, friendly or at least tolerant neighbors, and large numbers of "righteous gentiles." The maxim that derives from a lachrymose reading of Jewish history, "All the world is against us," is the most dangerous of the distortions that Baron wrote about.

David Hartman, who devoted his life to developing and defending a liberal version of Judaism and who inspired my colleagues' and my work on the Jewish tradition, described the choice facing Jews today as "Auschwitz or Sinai?" Sinai for him meant the covenant at the mountain and everything that followed from it—all the laws, interpretations, and arguments, the reiterated communal commitments, the work of the prophets, the rabbis, and the philosophers. But not only that: "Sinai requires us to believe in the possibility of integrating the moral demands of the prophets with the realism required for political survival." Morality enacted in the real world; realism constrained by moral demands: Hartman believed that Sinai qualifies us as agents. Auschwitz, by contrast, signifies eternal victimization.

I am a secular Jew, but I recognize that "secular" doesn't necessarily encompass "liberal." Although I believe that the ur-language of zealotry is religious, there have certainly been secular zealots—like those Spanish communists who, during the civil war, murdered priests and turned churches into stables. There are less brutal zealots also, who disdain belief and treat religious men and women as fools, the victims of priestcraft (which comes in many versions). By contrast, liberal secularists respect the lives that believers live and the communities they create, and work to guarantee the safety of both. They are also curious about religious faith. Some of the greatest scholars of the different religions have been liberal secularists.

In the world before secularism was possible, religious life was often bitterly contentious and a source of misery for those who lost out in the contests. The furtive remains of those miseries survive still, as in this story. An Israeli friend of mine, a secular and liberal Jew and a professor of philosophy, visited Spain and was taken around the city of Córdova by a Spanish colleague. Walking through the city, they approached an old, beautiful church. As they entered it, the Spaniard, a Catholic, mumbled a few words under his breath. My friend, startled, asked him to repeat the words more slowly and then said: "You have just uttered a Hebrew curse." The Spanish professor was, although he didn't know it, the distant descendent of Jews forced to convert and attend church services. For some time, perhaps for generations, his ancestors had remained secret Jews, and they recited the curse as a ritual disavowal of the service in which they were about to participate. The curse survived for centuries, although its meaning was lost. My secular Jewish friend felt no need to repeat it when he entered the church.

I don't know if the Catholic professor abandoned the curse after learning what it was or continued what had become a family tradition. There are religious Jews today who would never willingly visit a church, and there are religious Catholics who believe that the Jews should have converted long ago, since they have been abandoned by God. Old illiberal beliefs and believers are still with us. But there are also religious Jews and Catholics (and Protestants, Muslims, Hindus, and Buddhists) who merit the adjective "liberal." They are defined, I suspect, by the doctrines they reject, and here liberal Jews and Catholics and all the others would probably agree.

All of them would oppose the persecution and harassment of heretics and infidels. They might be saddened by the multiplication of denominations and sects, but they would never endorse state action to defend the faith they espoused. They would reject the use of coercion in religious matters; they wouldn't oppose, as their ancestors did, the maxim "Faith is free." They would not insist that their religious calendar shape everyone else's weeks and years. Liberal Jews, for example, would reject the claim that "Torah from Sinai" should determine the character and pace of Sabbath activity for all the inhabitants of the city or state—even if the state is Jewish.

More controversially, liberal believers would not open a shop on a public street, a street built and maintained by the city, and refuse to serve people whose religious or secular practices they disapproved of.

The right to refuse has recently been defended in the name of religious liberty. But refusal is a discriminatory act and possibly humiliating for the rejected customer, who has, like everyone else, been invited into the store. It can't be called liberal. Of course, believers (and anyone else) are free to form a private club and serve only members. But that freedom has nothing to do with religion—and liberal Jews (and the liberal others, too) would not want to join the club.

I suspect that men and women who are religiously liberal have difficulty with many aspects of the standard theologies of their faith. They would not accept the subordination of women. They would not believe the common teaching that the religion or irreligion of the "others" consigns them to eternal damnation. Liberal Jews would certainly not agree that most non-Jews will never see the world-to-come. Who knows whom we will encounter there? Liberal Protestants, even Evangelicals if the adjective "liberal" applies to them, would not agree that Jews are doomed to hellfire. Nor would any of the liberally religious join in efforts to forcefully establish the messianic kingdom or the Islamic caliphate or Jesus's holy commonwealth. I imagine them at least a little bit skeptical about the end time. How a "little bit" of skepticism fits with religious belief, I leave to the believers. Some of my friends, religious Jews, have no difficulty with the combination.

Liberal Jews live comfortably in a secular state that they also help to sustain. But it is important to say that illiberal Jews and illiberal members of every other religion can also live comfortably in a secular state even if they don't help to sustain it. They have only to give up the commitment that everyone else must live as they do. By contrast, liberal Jews cannot live comfortably in a state ruled by illiberal Jews—or, as in Iran today, by illiberal Muslims—where they would be subject to religious coercion. This is a common asymmetry. Liberal socialists cannot live comfortably in a state ruled by illiberal socialists, but illiberal socialists can live comfortably, can argue and organize freely, in a state ruled by liberal socialists. They have only to make their peace with the right of all the other groups to argue and organize. Perhaps the religious case is different: perhaps the concessions demanded from orthodox or fundamentalist men and women are more drastic than those required from the irreligious. Still, the point is general: the liberal secular state has been remarkably hospitable to people of every religious and ideological sort (not yet, obviously, to people of every racial and ethnic sort). In America, Jews have provided the critical test of that hospitality. In Israel today, and in many European countries, the treatment of Muslims is the critical test.

9
Who Is and Who Isn't?

Most Americans probably think that a liberal Jew or a liberal Catholic (or a liberal of any other faith) is a Jew or a Catholic who votes Democratic. That is partly right, since the adjective "liberal" is transferable, and liberal believers are likely to be liberal democrats and social democrats. In the United States, the Democratic Party has for many years been the favored home for men and women like that. But we have seen liberal Republicans (though recently only a few) who defend constitutional democracy, believe in an independent judiciary, feel comfortable in a pluralist society, and expect to rotate out of as well as into political office.

These are easy identifications. But how does the adjective "liberal" apply to historical figures who embody what we today take to be radical contradictions? Consider Voltaire, for example, who bravely defended religious liberty for Protestants in Catholic France but was at the same time a racist and anti-Semite. Or Thomas Jefferson, who fought for a constitutional republic and a bill of rights but owned slaves. Or John Stuart Mill, who argued beautifully for freedom of speech but supported colonialism, taking a paternalistic view of nations less "advanced" than his own. Or any number of writers (though not Mill) who defended liberty but assumed the subordination of women. The reputation of people like these is currently under attack; we are endlessly reminded of the sins of our forefathers and of our own failure to acknowledge the sins and to repair the damage they caused.

The failures are obvious, but I want to urge a more generous view of the forefathers (the foremothers are rarely criticized, although they shared the bigotries of their time). I take my cue from a line in the Bible about Noah, the man of the Flood. He was, says the biblical writer, "righteous in his generation." This has been taken to mean that Noah was only relatively righteous; he was not a man for all seasons or all ages. Among his contemporaries, he was a pretty good fellow. So Voltaire, in his generation, was a liberal *philosophe,* and Jefferson was a liberal republican, and Mill was the classic liberal liberal and something close to a liberal socialist. But if these men appeared among us today, with the contradictions of their generations, we would probably have to deny them the adjective.

Are there groups, parties, ideologies, and identities today that cannot be modified by the adjective "liberal"? Can there be, for example, liberal ultra-Orthodox Jews or liberal fundamentalist Christians? The adjectives sit uneasily together. Maybe talented and flexible individuals, if they were able to acknowledge the equal standing of women, could accommodate all the adjectives, but I suspect that their fellow believers would say that they had left the fold. Religious dogmatists, whatever the dogma, probably can't be liberal.

Can there be a liberal theocracy? Since this would be, it always has been, a regime ruled by men who claim to speak in God's name, the better question is, Can there be a liberal hierocracy—a liberal government of priests, ministers, rabbis, imams, or ayatolahs? Probably not; most men who speak in God's name insist upon their right to rule absolutely and are generally intolerant of dissent. Still, they sometimes imagine a liberal divinity and then a more liberal way of ruling—as the Talmudic sages did when they wrote that two contradictory legal opinions were both "words of the living God," or as sixteenth-century Protestants did when they insisted that "God's house has many mansions." More generally, however, liberal skepticism doesn't sit well with divine omniscience, or liberal irony with divine omnipotence.

There can't be liberal racists. So I believe, although in "woke" America a flood of books and articles describe and denounce the racism of (White) liberals. These beleaguered people are liberal democrats and liberal socialists who defend equality, civil liberties, and affirmative action but who harbor, it is said, racist impulses, emotions, and attitudes deep within. They are formal antiracists but not root-and-branch antiracists, so the root-and-branchers claim that they aren't antiracists at all. I don't agree, but I am not going to argue about that here—although I do want to remind readers of a line from the first Queen Elizabeth: "I would not make a window into men's souls to pinch them there." How do we know what lies deep within? Liberals don't go looking. So far as American politics is concerned, I am ready to make do with all the different kinds and degrees of antiracism. Perhaps, taken together, they will bring us closer to a post-racist society.

In any case, all I mean is that there can't be a version of racism that is liberal—and the same is true for anti-Semitism, Islamophobia, misogyny, and homophobia. Bigotry and hate don't have liberal versions. By contrast, there have been democratic and socialist racists, anti-Semites, and so on. Illiberalism is more common than it should be among those who are, at least formally, members of democratic and socialist parties. I have already quoted August Bebel's description of anti-Semitism as the "socialism of fools." In parts of Europe today, hatred of Muslims, promoted by right-wing populists, is the nationalism of fools.

Liberal Republicans can exist, even if they are not currently visible. I learned this early on; my closest friend in high school was the nephew of the local Republican Party boss. We disagreed about many things, none of which interfered with our friendship. Sometime in

1950, we went together to listen to Senator Joe McCarthy speaking at a nearby fairground. I was appalled and frightened; my friend was disgusted—different responses but both of them appropriately liberal.

There are liberal conservatives, too, most obviously those who try to conserve or rescue liberal democracy when it comes under attack—the Never Trumpers are the most recent example. Of course, we always have to ask what is being conserved. The effort to defend or revive hierarchical regimes can be a romantic project but not a liberal one.

I doubt that there can be a liberal capitalism given the inequalities that capitalism produces and the coercion it requires to keep workers in line. Capitalism under strong democratic and social democratic constraints might warrant the adjective—and so might a genuinely libertarian capitalism. Back in the 1970s, I taught a class, together with the libertarian philosopher Robert Nozick, called Capitalism and Socialism. The course was a semester-long debate. Nozick defended a version of free market capitalism where entrepreneurs, managers, and owners would get no coercive help from the state: no land seizures, no subsidies, no exemptions from safety and environmental rules, no tariffs, and no anti-union legislation. Without coercion and help of these kinds, he claimed, there would be far less inequality. Half seriously, he went on to say that a revolution to establish capitalism in the United States would be justified. But he was a capitalist revolutionary with no following among the capitalists.

There are liberal libertarians, of course, who agree (as Nozick would) that the laws of the market, however impressive, should not be constitutionally entrenched and that laissez-faire is only one possible social policy among others, however wise they think it is. Libertarianism is an ideology that is said to be liberal by definition. It often, but not always, is liberal in fact. We have seen some zealous libertarians in American politics in recent years.

Do all liberals merit the adjective? There are, I have to say, illiberal liberals—absolutists of different sorts who believe that their own version of liberalism is the last word. I have known liberal democrats and socialists who can't contain their contempt for their illiberal opponents. Yes, there are liberals who lack the generosity of spirit that I have been assuming defines us all.

I have already raised doubts about a liberal communist. The Stalinist version of communism certainly can't abide the adjective, but I am sure that there were liberal communists—in the nineteenth century, say—who believed in a plurality of communes of different sorts. More recently, too, some twentieth-century kibbutzniks were liberal (and some not). Communal life is sometimes rigidly ideological in character; sometimes it takes cultic forms, focused on a charismatic leader; sometimes it is an illiberal democracy, intolerant of dissidents. A liberal commune would have to have fairly easy entrances and exits, but it becomes less and less communal if people come and go.

There can certainly be liberal anticommunists, but during the Cold War there was also a fiercely illiberal anticommunism, most visibly represented by Senator Joe McCarthy, and some liberals were slow to recognize and condemn the illiberal version.

Whether there can be a liberal imperialism is doubtful, as I argued above, but there can be liberal civil servants of imperialism, people who study the culture of the natives and work to promote their independence or who oppose the daily humiliations that the servants of imperialism inflict on the people they rule. Think of Eric Blair, the future George Orwell, in Burma.

Fascists and Nazis can't be liberal, and they are usually eager to boast about their opposition to anything that might be qualified by the adjective. Totalitarianism is the ideal type of an illiberal politics.

There can't be a liberal police state, but there can be a liberal police force. I have a vivid memory of a political rally against the Suez war in Cambridge, England, in 1956. When the last speaker ended his lengthy peroration, the bobbies moved slowly into the crowd, saying, "It's all over. Please go home. It's all over. Please go home." I was amazed at this gentle behavior, quietly respectful of political dissent. But I might not have been similarly amazed had I been watching the police response to an antiwar rally in a working-class district of London or Manchester. That would be a better test of a liberal police force, and one that the police I know most often fail.

A liberal monarchy is possible, which is why we use the adjective "absolute" to describe the illiberal version. A liberal monarch rules alone and doesn't rotate in and out of office, but he or she recognizes a pluralist politics with constitutional restraints and a plurality of religions. I think that despotism can be enlightened, as some eighteenth-century despots claimed to be, but not liberal. Nor can tyranny live with a liberal modifier.

There can't be a liberal plutocracy; the defense of wealth is usually as brutal as it has to be. I am dubious about the possibility of a liberal oligarchy, but a liberal aristocracy is conceivable (along Jeffersonian lines) so long as membership is not hereditary. Competition in excellence and virtue and the social mobility it produces might have some of the features of rotation in office.

For all the nouns to which the adjective applies, it brings its various liberal qualifications: the constraint of political power; the defense of individual rights; the pluralism of parties, religions, and nations; the openness of civil society; the rights of opposition and disagreement; the accommodation of difference; the welcome of strangers. It brings generosity of spirit together with skepticism and irony. Critics of liberalism claim that these qualifications are often pushed too far, leaving a dangerously weakened or, in old English, emasculated democracy, or socialism, or Judaism. I agree that the adjective must not overwhelm the nouns, but I see little evidence of that. It is more important to stress the good work that the adjective does.

Finally, with regard to my own nouns, the ones dealt with in these chapters, liberal qualifications are critically important for contemporary politics. We need liberal democrats ready to fight against the new populism; liberal socialists who defend equality but oppose the frequent authoritarianism of left-wing regimes; liberal nationalists who resist contemporary xenophobic nationalisms, including those that are anti-Muslim and anti-Semitic; liberal internationalists who defend people in trouble across the border; liberal communitarians who oppose the exclusivist passions and fierce partisanship of some identity groups; liberal feminists who know when to use state power to promote gender equality and when not to; liberal professors who defend free speech on campuses; liberal intellectuals who not only "speak truth to power" but speak truth simply and always; and liberal Jews, Christians, Muslims, Hindus, Buddhists, and all the rest who stand against the unexpected return of religious zealotry. These battles for decency and truth are among the most important political battles of our time, and the adjective "liberal" is our most important weapon.

Bibliography

This is a list of the books, and a couple of articles, that were ready at hand during the Covid pandemic (plus a few books that I studied long ago). They were my pandemic companions; they helped me write this book. I have already named some of them in the text as a way of acknowledging special debts to their authors. Except for a few co-edited volumes, I haven't included any of my own books, although some of their arguments reappear in these chapters. The list is incomplete; it doesn't cover all my sources, not the ideas and sentences that were in my head or that I found on the Internet, only those on the pages in my study.

Amichai, Yehuda. *Great Tranquility: Questions and Answers.* Translated by Glenda Abramson and Tudor Parfit. New York: Harper and Row, 1983.

Baron, Salo W. *History and Jewish Historians: Essays and Addresses.* Compiled with a foreword by Arthur Hertzberg and Leon A. Feldman. Philadelphia: Jewish Publication Society of America, 1964.

Baxter, Richard. *The Holy Commonwealth.* London, 1659.

Bebel, August. *Women under Socialism.* 1879. Translated by Daniel DeLeon. New York: New York Labor News, 1906.

Benda, Julien. *The Treason of the Intellectuals.* 1927. Translated by Richard Aldington. New York: Routledge, 2017.

Bobbio, Norberto. *Left and Right: The Significance of a Political Distinction.* Translated by Allan Cameron. Cambridge, UK: Polity Press, 1996.

Bynum, Caroline Walker, and Michael Walzer, co-chairs. *Report of the Committee on the Status of Women in the Faculty of Arts and Sciences.* Harvard University, Cambridge, MA, April 1971.

Coser, Lewis A. *Greedy Institutions: Patterns of Undivided Commitment.* New York: Free Press, 1974.

Coser, Lewis A. "Sects and Sectarianism," *Dissent* (Autumn 1954).

Dewey, John. *Democracy and Education.* New York: Macmillan, 1961.

Gramsci, Antonio. *Selections from the Prison Notebooks.* Edited by Quinton Hoare and Geoffrey Nowell Smith. New York: International Publishers, 1971.

Greenberg, Hayim. *The Essential Hayim Greenberg: Essays and Addresses on Jewish Culture, Socialism, and Zionism.* Edited by Mark A. Raider. Tuscaloosa: University of Alabama Press, 2016.

Hartman, David. "Auschwitz or Sinai," *Jerusalem Post,* December 12, 1982.

Haslett, Tobi. "Magic Actions: Looking Back at the George Floyd Revolution," *n+1* (Summer 2021).

Hobbes, Thomas. *Leviathan.* With an introduction by A. D. Lindsay. New York: E. P. Dutton, 1950.

Howe, Irving. *A Margin of Hope: An Intellectual Autobiography.* New York: Harcourt Brace Jovanovich, 1982.

Howe, Irving. *Selected Writings, 1950–1990.* New York: Harcourt Brace Jovanovich, 1990.

Kirsch, Adam. *Why Trilling Matters.* New Haven: Yale University Press, 2011.

Kundera, Milan. *The Unbearable Lightness of Being.* Translated by Michael Henry Heim. New York: Harper Colophon Books, 1984.

Levine, Philip. *7 Years from Somewhere.* New York: Atheneum, 1979.

Makiya, Kanan. *The Rope: A Novel.* New York: Pantheon, 2016.

Mantel, Hilary. *The Mirror and the Light.* New York: Henry Holt, 2020.

Mantena, Karuna. "Another Realism: The Politics of Gandhian Nonviolence," *The American Political Science Review* 106, no. 2 (May 2012).

Marshall, T. H. *Class, Citizenship, and Social Development: Essays.* With an introduction by S. M. Lipset. New York: Praeger, 1973.

Mazzini, Guiseppe. *A Cosmopolitanism of Nations: Writings on Democracy, Nation-Building, and Internationalism.* Edited by Stefano Recchia and Nadia Urbinati. Translated by Stefano Recchia. Princeton: Princeton University Press, 2009.

Miller, David. *On Nationality.* Oxford: Clarendon Press, 1995.

Miłosz, Czeław. *The Captive Mind*. 1953. Translated by Jane Zielonko. New York: Vintage, 1990.

Nafisi, Azar. *Reading Lolita in Tehran: A Memoir in Books*. New York: Random House, 2003.

Neale, J. E. *Queen Elizabeth*. New York: Harcourt Brace Jovanovich, 1934.

Nove, Alec. "Feasible Socialism?" *Dissent* (Summer 1985).

Okin, Susan Moller. *Is Multiculturalism Bad for Women?* Edited by Martha Nussbaum. Princeton: Princeton University Press, 1999.

Okin, Susan Moller. *Justice, Gender, and the Family*. New York: Basic Books, 1989.

Okin, Susan Moller. *Women in Western Political Thought*. Princeton: Princeton University Press, 1979.

Orwell, George. *The Collected Essays, Journalism, and Letters*. Edited by Sonia Orwell and Ian Angus. 4 volumes. New York: Harcourt Brace World, 1968.

Rosenblum, Nancy. *Good Neighbors: The Democracy of Everyday Life in America*. Princeton: Princeton University Press, 2016.

Rosselli, Carlo. *Liberal Socialism*. Edited and with an introduction by Nadia Urbinati. Translated by William McCuaig. Princeton: Princeton University Press, 1994.

Rousseau, Jean-Jacques. *The Government of Poland*. Translated by Willmore Kendall. New York: Bobbs-Merrill, 1972.

Rousseau, Jean-Jacques. *The Social Contract*. Translated by G. D. H. Cole. New York: E. P. Dutton, 1950.

Schultz, Philip. *Deep within the Ravine: Poems*. New York: Penguin Books, 1974.

Shklar, Judith. *Ordinary Vices*. Cambridge, MA: Belknap/Harvard University Press, 1984.

Smith, Steven B. *Reclaiming Patriotism in an Age of Extremes*. New Haven: Yale University Press, 2021.

Stolzenberg, Nomi M., and David N. Myers. *American Shtetl: The Making of Kiryas Joel, a Hasidic Village in Upstate New York*. Princeton: Princeton University Press, 2022.

Szymborska, Wisława. *Sounds, Feelings, Thoughts: Seventy Poems*. Translated and introduced by Magnus I. Krynski and Robert A. Maguire. Princeton: Princeton University Press, 1981.

Tamir, Yael. *Liberal Nationalism.* Princeton: Princeton University Press, 1995.

Tawney, R. H. *RHT's Commonplace Book.* Edited by J. M. Winter and D. M. Joslin. Cambridge: Cambridge University Press, 1972.

Walzer, Michael, Menachem Lorberbaum, and Noam J. Zohar, eds. *The Jewish Political Tradition:* Volume I, *Authority;* Volume II, *Membership;* Volume III, *Community;* Volume IV, *Politics in History.* New Haven: Yale University Press, 2000–.

Walzer, Michael, and Nicolaus Mills. *Getting Out: Historical Perspectives on Leaving Iraq.* Philadelphia: University of Pennsylvania Press, 2006.

Whitman, Walt. *Leaves of Grass.* New York: Harper and Brothers, 1950.

Williams, C. K. *Repair: Poems.* New York: Farrar, Straus, and Giroux, 1999.

Index